Welcome to Windows 8

Not since home computing was truly put on the map with the launch of Windows 95 has Microsoft delivered such a radical overhaul to its world-conquering operating system.

Having witnessed the mainstream popularity of tablet devices, particularly the Apple iPad, Microsoft has responded with a version of Windows that spans the whole gamut of computing devices: desktops, laptops, tablets – and hybrids of all three. It's an operating system designed for touchscreen and non-touch devices, and hardware new and old. For the first time, it's even designed to power Microsoft's own computer, Surface.

Windows 8 has a battery of new features. The new "Modern UI" Start menu, the Windows Store, the touchscreen controls, the death of the Windows Start button – it's hard to know which monumental change to the operating system to start with. Fortunately, we've got them all covered in this guide – and much more.

This MagBook carefully explains all the major new features in Windows 8. Where applicable, we've also written step-by-step walkthroughs to help you get to grips with those features and new ways of working. Dotted throughout the book, you'll find annotated guides to the new-look Windows Start menu, the revamped desktop, the touch controls and the new Settings menus, so that you can sit with this guide in front of you and (literally, in the case of tablet owners) feel your way around the operating system.

As with any modern operating system, apps are a critical part of Windows 8. We help you familiarise yourself with several of the new-style apps Microsoft has pre-installed on every Windows 8 Start menu, then delve into Windows Store to single out 20 of our favourite apps you can download – in many cases, completely free of charge.

Windows 8 also has plenty to offer Windows traditionalists who have no interest in apps and modern tablet hardware. We explain how to master Microsoft's new take on the traditional Windows desktop, highlighting the new Task Manager and other advanced features aimed at power users, such as mounting ISOs and VHDs.

Finally, you'd be foolish to think about upgrading to a new operating system without thinking about security – and rest assured, we won't leave you unprotected. We've got a whole chapter dealing with securing your Windows 8 PC, which for the first time comes with built-in antivirus software. Should you trust it? We've got a rundown of the alternative security suites to help you reach your own conclusion and decide on the best security solution for your specific needs.

Using Windows 8 for the first time can be a disorienting experience. Daunting, even. We hope this guide will make those tentative first steps a great deal easier.

Barry Collins
Editor, Ultimate Guide to Windows 8
editor@pcpro.co.uk

Contents

INTRO   page 6   **30 best features** *From the Modern UI to built-in antivirus, the 30 key reasons why now is the right time to upgrade to Windows 8*

CHAPTER 1   page 12   **Buying Windows 8** *Choosing the right edition • Upgrading from Windows 7 • 8 reasons to buy a Windows 8 tablet*

CHAPTER 2   page 26   **Your new-look Windows** *The Windows 8 Start screen • Charms and search • Personalising Windows 8 • Picture passwords*

CHAPTER 3   page 42   **Introducing Modern apps** *Mail, People and Calendar • Music and Video • Bing Maps and Search • 20 of the best Modern apps*

CHAPTER 4   page 60   **The Windows desktop** *Personalise the desktop • Advanced shortcuts • Mastering Jump Lists • The Task Manager*

CHAPTER 5   page 74   **Advanced features** *Disk images • BitLocker • Secure Boot • Windows To Go • Extend battery life • Accessibility features*

1 Buying Windows 8

BUYING WINDOWS 8

Windows 8 marks a major departure for Microsoft. The mouse and keyboard basics remain largely in place, but with touchscreen devices so prevalent these days Microsoft has added a whole new layer to Windows 8 to take full advantage – the Modern UI. This colourful grid interface gives a totally different user experience, perfect for use on the move. These new features, while both innovative and useful, in some ways make it more difficult to choose which version of Windows 8 suits you. In this chapter we look at the different editions of Windows 8, we show you how to go about upgrading your PC, and we give eight reasons why you might want to buy a shiny new Windows 8 tablet to enjoy Microsoft's new OS in its full glory.

2 Introducing Modern UI

YOUR NEW-LOOK WINDOWS

Microsoft has pushed the desktop to the background in Windows 8, introducing a new Start screen designed to be used across PCs, laptops and tablets. This full-screen interface is built around large, bright tiles which serve as gateways to your applications and folders. Some are even alive with information, dynamically updating themselves with the latest news headlines, weather information and notifications from your email accounts. The radically redesigned Start screen has its own settings menus, search options and even a new toolbar, dubbed the Charms bar. We cover them all in this section, plus we look at how to personalise the Start screen – from changing its colour scheme to creating your own live tiles.

3 Modern apps

INTRODUCING MODERN APPS

Windows 8 introduces a whole new class of apps to the operating system. Previously known as "Metro style apps", but now merely referred to as Modern apps, these are more akin to the small, lightweight apps found on smartphones and rival tablets than the full-blown Windows apps of yesteryear. In this chapter, we'll introduce you to the Modern apps that come pre-installed with Windows 8 and explain how to get the most from them. We'll also introduce you to the Windows Store, where you can find thousands more apps to download and install yourself. Finally, we'll pick our 20 favourite apps from the Windows Store to give you a flavour of what you can do with your new Windows 8 device.

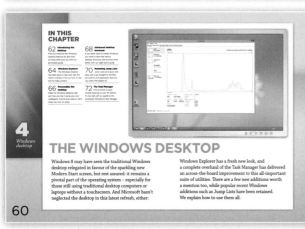

4 Windows desktop

THE WINDOWS DESKTOP

Windows 8 may have seen the traditional Windows desktop relegated in favour of the sparkling new Modern Start screen, but rest assured: it remains a pivotal part of the operating system – especially for those still using traditional desktop computers or laptops without a touchscreen. And Microsoft hasn't neglected the desktop in this latest refresh, either: Windows Explorer has a fresh new look, and a complete overhaul of the Task Manager has delivered an across-the-board improvement to this all-important suite of utilities. There are a few new additions worth a mention too, while popular recent Windows additions such as Jump Lists have been retained. We explain how to use them all.

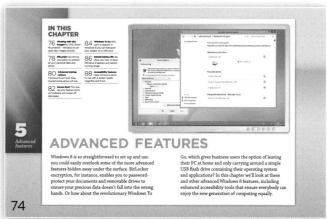

5 Advanced features

ADVANCED FEATURES

Windows 8 is so straightforward to set up and use you could easily overlook some of the more advanced features hidden away under the surface. BitLocker encryption, for instance, enables you to password-protect your documents and removable drives to ensure your precious data doesn't fall into the wrong hands. Or how about the revolutionary Windows To Go, which gives business users the option of leaving their PC at home and only carrying around a simple USB flash drive containing their operating system and applications? In this chapter we'll look at these and other advanced Windows 8 features, including enhanced accessibility tools that ensure everybody can enjoy the new generation of computing equally.

CHAPTER 6 page 90 **Internet and networking** *Introducing Internet Explorer 10 • HomeGroup • Setting up a wireless network • Using 3G on tablets*

CHAPTER 7 page 100 **Handling files and folders** *Files and folders: the basics • Mastering libraries • Microsoft SkyDrive*

CHAPTER 8 page 108 **Security** *Backing up your data • Family Safety • Action Center • Windows Defender • Windows Firewall • User Account Control*

CHAPTER 9 page 130 **Windows 8 on tablets** *Touchscreen gestures • Mastering the onscreen keyboard • Handwriting recognition*

CHAPTER 10 page 138 **Entertainment** *DVD and Blu-ray playback • Windows Media Player • Windows 8 and the Xbox 360 • Playing games*

CHAPTER 11 page 148 **Windows jargon explained** *Our A-to-Z glossary of terminology you might encounter while using or upgrading to Windows 8*

6
Internet & networking

INTERNET AND NETWORKING

We're now in a connected world, where tablets are used to browse the internet as much as the PC or laptop. Windows 8 caters for all users, so in this chapter we'll show you how to get up and running online – both on the internet and on your home network. However you use Windows, you'll need a web browser, so we start with a look at Microsoft's new Internet Explorer 10

browser – in both touch and desktop versions. We'll explain how to set up a wireless network at home, and connect your PC or tablet to it with maximum speed and security. We'll examine the HomeGroup features for easily sharing your files across multiple PCs, and we'll look at how you can use 3G to get online on your new Windows 8 tablet when you're out and about.

90

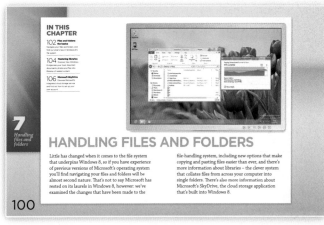

7
Handling files and folders

HANDLING FILES AND FOLDERS

Little has changed when it comes to the file system that underpins Windows 8, so if you have experience of previous versions of Microsoft's operating system you'll find navigating your files and folders will be almost second nature. That's not to say Microsoft has rested on its laurels in Windows 8, however; we've examined the changes that have been made to the

file-handling system, including new options that make copying and pasting files easier than ever, and there's more information about libraries – the clever system that collates files from across your computer into single folders. There's also more information about Microsoft's SkyDrive, the cloud storage application that's built into Windows 8.

100

8
Security

SECURITY

Windows 8 contains a wealth of features for ensuring things run smoothly and stably. In this chapter we'll look at ways to restore your PC when things go wrong, and how to back up your valuable files using the new File History feature. We'll also look at using Family Safety to ensure your children stay safe online; and we introduce the Action Center, which can give you

an early warning if something's not right. We'll show you how Windows Defender and the Windows Firewall keep you safe from viruses and cyber-attacks, and how to configure them to work the way you want. We also explain how Windows 8's User Account Control system prevents your settings being changed, and look at the best third-party security software that's out there.

108

9
Windows 8 on tablets

WINDOWS 8 ON TABLETS

Microsoft has completely revamped the Windows interface in its biggest interface overhaul since Windows 95. The force behind that change is the emergent popularity of tablets. In this chapter we'll show you how the new look works on the devices it was designed for. You'll discover how to get around the front end quickly using a selection of swipes, taps and

Microsoft's ingenious edge gestures. We'll unveil the power of the Windows 8 touch keyboard, which allows you to type emails and documents almost as quickly as on a laptop or desktop keyboard. And we'll show you how Microsoft's superlative handwriting recognition technology, coupled with a stylus and digitiser pen, takes text entry to the next level.

130

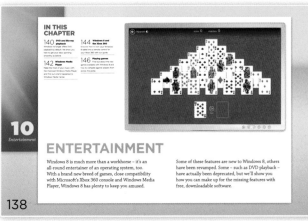

10
Entertainment

ENTERTAINMENT

Windows 8 is much more than a workhorse – it's an all-round entertainer of an operating system, too. With a brand new breed of games, close compatibility with Microsoft's Xbox 360 console and Windows Media Player, Windows 8 has plenty to keep you amused.

Some of these features are new to Windows 8, others have been revamped. Some – such as DVD playback – have actually been deprecated, but we'll show you how you can make up for the missing features with free, downloadable software.

138

11
Glossary of terms

Windows jargon explained

150

The 30 best features

THE TOUCH INTERFACE IS THE MOST OBVIOUS NEW FEATURE IN WINDOWS 8.
BUT DELVE A LITTLE DEEPER AND YOU'LL FIND THERE'S SOMETHING FOR EVERYONE

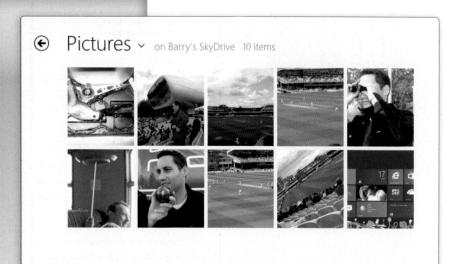

3. BUILT-IN ANTIVIRUS Windows 8 is the first version of Windows to come with built-in antivirus protection – and not before time. Microsoft Security Essentials, the optional free antivirus package for older versions of Windows, now appears under the Windows Defender umbrella in Windows 8. As with the Windows 7 version of MSE, it's fairly light on features, but for an unobtrusive minder that keeps an eye out for anything untoward on your system, it should suffice.

4. NO NEED FOR NEW HARDWARE As with Windows 7, Microsoft isn't raising the hardware requirements for its latest operating system. That means – in theory – any PC capable of running Windows Vista should be able to handle Windows 8. In other words, any PC bought in the past three to four years should cope.

5. AIRPLANE MODE With Windows 8, there is no more scrambling around for Wi-Fi/Bluetooth switches. A new option in the Settings menu allows you to put your tablet or laptop into Airplane Mode, just like a smartphone, meaning there's absolutely no danger that you're going to send your easyJet flight catapulting into the South Terminal at Gatwick. Not that there was much chance in the first place...

6. SKYDRIVE INTEGRATION Microsoft's cloud computing service allows you to save gigabytes of files on the company's servers for free! The SkyDrive app on the Windows 8 Start menu provides access to any documents, photos and music you've already uploaded to Microsoft's cloud service, and allows you to upload new files. SkyDrive also appears in Windows Explorer on the desktop, allowing you to drag and drop files to it as if it were a hard disk on your own PC.

1. LIVE TILES The Modern UI Start Screen may not be everyone's cup of tea, but it does have undeniable benefits, chief of which are the live tiles. Unlike certain other mobile OSes – yes, we're looking at you Apple – Windows 8's Modern UI icons do more than merely open the app. They provide a rich stream that turns the Windows Start screen into a dashboard teeming with live data.

The interactive tile for the Mail application provides snippets from unread inbox messages; the Music tile shows which track is currently playing; the Calendar app shows forthcoming diary appointments. Set it up properly and it provides an overview of everything you need to know when firing up your PC or tablet first thing in the morning.

2. TASK MANAGER Nobody really likes spending time in Task Manager, but should you be forced to, the utility's new look in Windows 8 makes it a darn sight easier.

Microsoft has introduced the elegant simplicity of heat-mapping to help identify apps that may be hogging CPU cycles or memory, while a range of new performance graphs gives you instant visual notification if your CPU, memory or network connection is taking an unexpected hit.

# of Windows 8

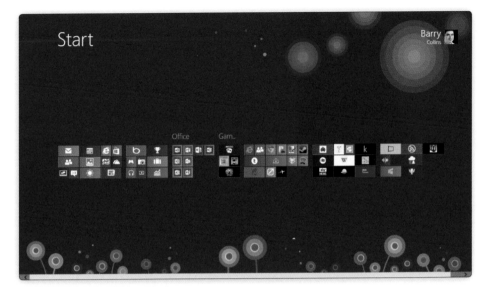

Start

Barry
Collins

Office   Gam...

12. APPS SHARING DATA Unlike other operating systems, Windows 8 apps can freely exchange data with one another. You could, for example, allow a Twitter client to have access to your Photos app, allowing you to pick a photo and share it via the micro-blogging service simply by opening the Share charm on the left-hand side of the screen and selecting the Twitter app. Likewise, you could pick a handful of photos and have them opened in a photo-editing app.

7. TILE GROUPING Install a few apps from the Windows Store and the Start screen can start to look disorganised. However, apps can be arranged into customisable groups – Games, Work, Music, for example – simply by dragging and dropping them into position. Once your apps are in place, click on the little minus sign in the bottom-right corner, or pinch to zoom out if you're working on a touchscreen, and you get a helicopter-style view of your Start screen. Right-click on a particular group of apps and you can give it a name.

8. WINDOWS STORE The Windows Store contains thousands of apps, many of them free, for your Windows 8 device. The Store is cleanly presented, with apps sensibly broken down into categories and sortable by highest rating, most recently added and other criteria. Many publishers offer time-limited trial versions of their apps before you have to buy, and apps are sold on a per-customer rather than a per-PC basis, so you can install them on multiple devices.

9. INTERACTIVE LOCK SCREEN No longer is the Windows lock screen little more than a glorified password prompt. The new-look Lock screen can now include snippets of information like the number of unread emails you have, or the state of the battery. To unlock your PC, simply swipe upwards on a tablet device, or click and drag the screen skywards on a laptop or desktop.

10. SPLIT-SCREEN APPS While other mobile OSes boast of multitasking, Windows 8 actually does it in a meaningful way. Apps can be run split-screen, with three quarters of the screen devoted to one app and a thin slice down either side of the screen afforded to another. For example, you can browse the web in Internet Explorer 10 while keeping the People app open on the right side of the screen, delivering live updates from your social networks.

11. TOUCH KEYBOARDS Nobody can accuse Microsoft of not putting enough thought into its soft keyboard for touchscreen users. There are two different types on offer: one that spans the full width of the screen, or a split keyboard that makes it easier to type on larger tablet screens. The split keyboard can be zoomed to different sizes, and cleverly places the number keys in between the two banks of letters, leaving them easily accessible but not in the way. In addition to the two soft keyboard options, Windows 8 also offers handwriting recognition, enabling stylus users to write into web forms, the browser bar or jot notes.

13. FEWER SURPRISE RESTARTS A welcome change introduced by Windows 8 is that your PC shouldn't surprise you by suddenly restarting to install a security update any more.

Microsoft promises only to restart for security patches once a month – unless a "critical security update" crops up, in which case Microsoft will push out an update and restart machines. Secondly, there will be no more pop-ups interrupting presentations or DVD playback – Microsoft will instead put a prominent warning about necessary restarts on the revamped Lock screen. You'll also get three days' notice of any restart, not the 20-minute countdown you get with Windows 7. Even if you sail past that deadline, Windows 8 will not restart if you have applications running or unsaved work.

ndy murray

BING DAILY
TOP STORY

**7/7 VICTIM
ACHIEVES PARALYMPIC DREAM**

KLOCHKOV

MSN UK 3 HOURS AGO

Martine Wright, who lost both her legs after being horrifically injured in the 7/7 bombings, describes her 'goosebumps' after representing her country at the Paralympics.

on the chosen photo – tapping each of your kids in age order, for example – and that becomes your Windows login. Should you forget your Picture Password, you can switch straight back to the conventional text-based login.

18. INSTANT SEARCH Instead of having to scroll through dozens of tiles to find the app you're looking for, Windows 8 lets you simply start typing the name of your desired app on the main Start screen. In the bat of an eyelid, the search returns a list of matching apps for you to choose from: it could barely be easier once you're used to it.

Windows 8 Search has much more to offer than that, though. Aside from searching for specific apps, you can also search for settings and files stored on your PC. It's also possible to search within individual apps: it's simple to find songs by a particular artist in the Music app, for instance, or beef recipes using the Bewise Cookbook app.

19. USER ACCOUNTS Windows 8 is the first tablet OS to offer different user accounts on the same device, so the kids can't get access to mum and dad's apps, email and documents if you're sharing a tablet in the home.

20. SECURE BOOT This anti-malware measure will prevent malicious software from starting before Windows 8 is up and running. It's designed to head off rootkits and other forms of malware that attempt to hijack the startup process.

21. REVAMPED EXPLORER Although on the surface the traditional Windows desktop is almost identical to that of Windows 7, changes have been made under the skin. Windows Explorer is now graced with the ribbon interface that first arrived with Office 2007 and has slowly made its way across almost all of Microsoft's applications.

The ribbon sports sizeable buttons for common tasks such as Copy, Paste and Rename. Microsoft claims it's relied upon years of Windows telemetry to determine which functions are given greater emphasis. The Explorer ribbon also hides tabs until they're relevant. Click on a JPG in an Explorer menu and the Picture Tools tab appears, for example, allowing you to set a photo as your desktop background or rotate the photo left or right.

14. CROSS-DEVICE SYNCHRONISATION The Windows 8 installation screen all but forces you to set up a Windows Live account. This not only becomes the login for your PC and gives you access to the Windows Store, it allows you to synchronise settings across different Windows 8 devices.

Your lock screen, desktop wallpaper and Modern UI theme are all synchronised by default, providing visual consistency across devices. Browsing history, bookmarks and other Windows settings are also shared, while the Sync menu lets you synchronise certain app settings.

15. IMPROVED 3G SUPPORT Windows 8 offers support for 3G and forthcoming 4G networks, including built-in meters to make sure consumers and business users don't stray past their data cap. Hefty device drivers won't download by default whilst running on mobile broadband, and the new Task Manager reveals which apps are hogging your data connection, allowing you to kill the most greedy. Windows 8 will also automatically switch to Wi-Fi when in range of a known access point to prevent running up unnecessary bills.

16. RUN ISO IMAGES Windows 8 throws a meaty bone to power users, namely the ability to run ISO files natively. You can, for example, download the ISO of a Linux distro or another piece of software to the Windows desktop, double-click to "mount" the file, and run the SETUP.EXE without having to physically burn the ISO to disc. Not only will this save you having to keep a supply of blank DVDs to hand, but also provides the performance boost of running from a local hard disk/SSD, rather than an optical drive.

17. PICTURE PASSWORDS Tapping in passwords on a tablet, even using Microsoft's excellent soft keyboard, is less than ideal. Picture Passwords are an inventive alternative: you pick a photo from your library, draw three gestures with your finger

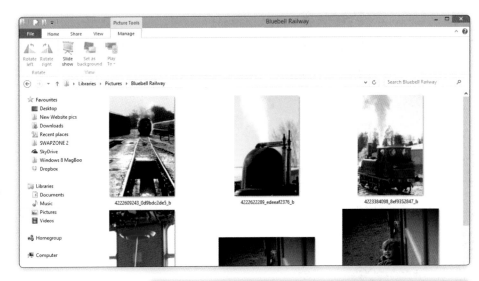

Clockwise from top left: Picture Passwords allow you to secure a tablet device without typing in fiddly passwords; the revamped Windows Explorer includes the ribbon menu for the first time; Refresh Your PC cleans your computer without deleting personal files; the Kinect controller is heading to the PC; and the new Search tool makes it a doddle to find installed apps.

22. REFRESH PC We all have *those* relatives – the ones who install every toolbar, utility and Facebook app they can point a mouse at, and then wonder why their PC is so slow. With Windows 8, however, Microsoft has eased the pain of a full reinstall with a new feature called Restore PC.

This leaves all your files, settings and apps downloaded from the Windows Store intact, and clears out the rest. Yes, this does mean that Windows desktop software will need to be reinstalled, but it's less painful than starting from a completely clean installation.

23. THUMBNAIL PREVIEWS Hover your mouse over the top-left corner of the Start screen and a column of thumbnails appears, allowing you to select any application currently being used on your PC. Touchscreen users can merely flick their finger from the left-hand edge of the screen to scroll through the open apps.

24. KINECT FOR WINDOWS Forgive us for a little crystal ball gazing, as we've yet to see a Windows 8 system running with Microsoft's gesture-based controller, but the potential marriage of Kinect and the new interface is too enormous to ignore.

The new interface was patently designed for touch controls, and few will want to sit prodding at a large, vertical touchscreen on their desktop. But if it were possible to scroll through the Start screen with a casual wave of the hand, rotate a photo with a flick of your wrist, or skip to the next track with the brush of finger... Well, suddenly Windows 8 would become a more compelling proposition on the desktop. It's a feature Microsoft is working on.

25. RESET PC Unlike the gentler Refresh PC (see above), Reset PC provides an automated way to completely wipe your Windows 8 installation and start from scratch –

handy if you're planning to sell on your PC with the operating system intact.

There are two types of Restore available: a "thorough" clean that removes all of your applications and data and makes them irrecoverable by writing over the deleted files several times. Then there's the "quick" clean that effectively just formats the drive and reinstalls the OS, which is the option to pick if you're merely wiping your own PC.

26. USB 3 SUPPORT Microsoft promises that Windows 8 will provide native support for every USB 3 drive and device on the market, while of course retaining compatibility with the older USB 2 and 1 devices. However, there has been no word as yet on native support for the potentially much faster Thunderbolt technology.

27. PANORAMIC BACKGROUNDS Windows 8 allows you to stretch one panoramic background image across two screens. This only works on screens of the same size and resolution, though.

28. FASTER BOOT TIMES Microsoft claims to have made Windows 8 boot

times up to 70% faster than those of Windows 7 by making subtle changes to the way the PC shuts down and resumes. Windows also now takes advantage of all available processor cores, reducing boot times on today's multi-core systems.

29. FILE COPY CHARTS The new file copy dialog is a small fillip for anyone who frequently shunts large files from drive to drive. Click "more details" in the dialog box, and a little graph appears displaying variations in transfer speed and the average speed in MB/sec, which is pleasingly geeky. Should you find the file transfer is bogging down your system, you can now pause the transfer, finish what you're doing, then resume where you left off. Sometimes it's the little things...

30. WINDOWS TO GO One you might see at work. Windows To Go allows companies to provide employees with a locked-down installation of Windows 8 on a USB thumb drive. This means you could be given a USB stick with all the company's applications pre-installed, which you could then run securely on your PC at home, without having to install any software on your own PC.

MAG**BOOK**

The Ultimate Guide to
Windows® Phone

Tips, tricks
and shortcuts
for the new
Windows Phone

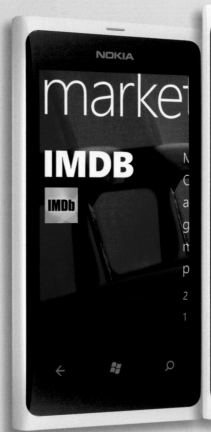

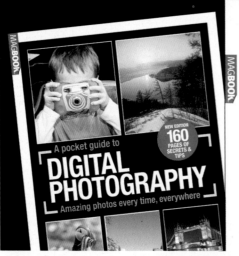
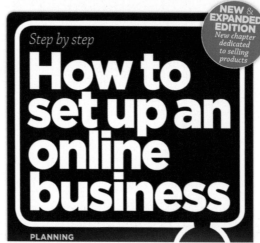
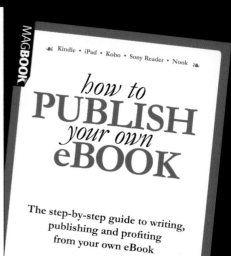

IN THIS CHAPTER

14 Choosing the right edition of Windows 8

There are three main versions of Windows 8, but choosing the one that best meets your needs is easier that ever before. We guide you through the process.

18 Upgrading from Windows 7

Windows 8 makes it easy to upgrade your system from Windows 7 – or even Windows Vista or XP if you have an older system. We run you through the process.

22 Windows 8 vs Windows RT There's a new version of Windows 8 designed primarily for tablets. We look at the differences, and what kind of devices you'll find running it.

24 8 reasons to buy a Windows 8 tablet

Windows 8 is designed to make the most of touch devices, so we look at the new features that may sway you towards a tablet purchase.

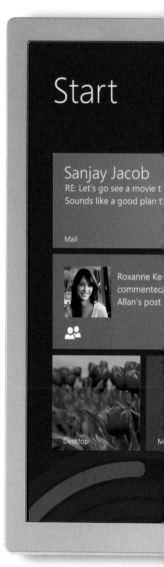

1
Buying Windows 8

BUYING WINDO

Windows 8 marks a major departure for Microsoft. The mouse and keyboard basics remain largely in place, but with touchscreen devices so prevalent these days, Microsoft has added a whole new layer to Windows 8 to take full advantage – the Modern UI. This colourful grid interface gives a totally different user experience, perfect for use on the move. These new features, while

WS 8

both innovative and useful, in some ways make it more difficult to choose which version of Windows 8 suits you. In this chapter we look at the different editions of Windows 8, we show you how to go about upgrading your PC, and we give eight reasons why you might want to buy a shiny new Windows 8 tablet to enjoy Microsoft's new OS in its full glory.

THERE ARE SEVERAL VERSIONS OF WINDOWS 8 TO CHOOSE FROM, BUT FOR PERSONAL USE THE DECISION IS VERY SIMPLE

Choosing the right version

If the various editions of Windows 7 confused you, there's good news: with Windows 8 things are much simpler. Gone is the stripped down Starter edition, and you're spared having to work out what makes the Ultimate edition better than Home Premium.

With Windows 8, Microsoft has thankfully narrowed the range down to only three publicly available versions: Windows 8, Windows 8 Pro and Windows RT. For PC users, the first two are the main ones to choose from. The third option – Windows RT – is a bit special, for reasons we'll go into a little later.

The good news is that this newly streamlined approach is reflected in Microsoft's Windows 8 pricing strategy too, and in general it's a change for the better. While putting Windows 7 on a PC cost upwards of £100 in some cases, Windows 8 is an absolute steal by comparison: you can now upgrade from an existing PC for £24.99.

WINDOWS 8 The main version, and the one the vast majority of people will want, is simply called Windows 8. It comes with all the core features of the operating system that you'll find detailed throughout this guide, including the all-new Start screen, access to the Windows Store packed with downloadable apps to go with the bundled selection, the new File History feature and the familiar Windows desktop. It's also the version most likely to be installed on a new PC or laptop. If you mainly use your PC for getting online, doing a bit of work and playing games – as most people do – this version has everything you need.

WINDOWS 8 PRO The Pro version contains almost everything that's in the standard version of Windows 8, plus several important extras aimed specifically at enthusiasts and business users. These include encryption features for keeping your important files secure, virtualisation abilities, and some management and connectivity extras. What it doesn't include as standard is Windows Media Player, but you can easily download it as an add-on if required.

The £15 upgrade offer

Microsoft wants as many people as possible running its new software, so if you've bought a PC or laptop in the past few months, you can upgrade it to Windows 8 at a lower price than everyone else. Any Windows 7 system bought between 2 June 2012 and 31 January 2013 will qualify for the offer. Just register at windowsupgradeoffer.com, and you can upgrade to Windows 8 Pro for £14.99.

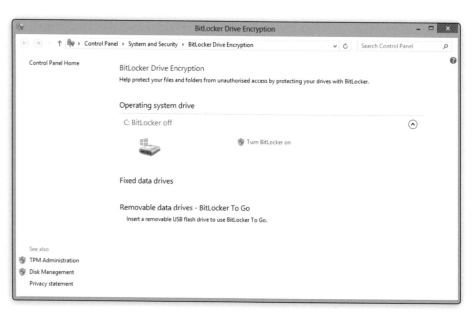

Windows 8 Pro comes with several extras aimed at the business user, including drive encryption to protect your important files.

The new-look Windows 8 Start screen has been designed specifically with touchscreens in mind.

The majority of home users won't need any of these advanced tools, so for the purposes of a family laptop or a gaming PC you can safely rule out the Pro version from your thinking. However, if your PC or laptop is used in an office environment, or for key business duties, the additional cost of Windows 8 Pro may prove to be a wise investment. Some users also simply like the luxury of having all the features an operating system can offer, so you can be sure Windows 8 Pro will be popular with enthusiasts.

Strictly speaking, there is another version to be aware of – Windows 8 Enterprise – but you can ignore that one. It's largely the same as Windows 8 Pro, but is available only through certain Microsoft business schemes. You won't see it in stores, and it won't be offered to consumers online.

RETAIL OR UPGRADE? Unlike with previous versions of Windows, you won't actually be able to buy a full retail version of Windows 8 in the shops. The Upgrade edition is as close as you'll get, which is in effect an acknowledgement that the vast majority of people looking to buy Windows 8 will already be running Windows. Upgrading can be carried out without deleting your existing files, and it's also very affordable, as the table overleaf shows.

Of course, any new PC or laptop that you buy will come with Windows 8 pre-installed and ready to go, but there is one other option that will appeal to those who want the experience of being able to install Windows 8 fresh – or the closest thing to it, anyway. Replacing the full boxed product will be something called a Personal Use License

The 64-bit question

There are two functionally identical versions of each Windows 8 installer: one for a 32-bit version of the OS; one for a 64-bit version. Choose wisely at the start; there's no way to switch between the two versions without wiping your system and running a clean install.

The choice depends on the hardware on which you're installing Windows. The 32-bit version of Windows 8 will work on pretty much any PC, however old, and it all but guarantees compatibility with old components that may not have 64-bit drivers, and with old software such as classic games and business applications. The problem is that it can only use a maximum of 4GB of RAM, limiting your scope to upgrade your system in the future.

The 64-bit edition lets you install more RAM, so it's the better choice in the long term, and it may also offer slight performance benefits in intensive software. For this reason, most new PCs and laptops bought today come with the 64-bit software pre-installed. It won't, however, work on some older hardware.

You needn't worry about installing the wrong version, as an upgrade compatibility checker is built into the Windows 8 setup process. If you try to install the 64-bit version on hardware that doesn't support it, the setup checker will tell you to switch to the 32-bit version.

Note, if you're upgrading from an older 32-bit version of Windows, you can't move directly to 64-bit Windows 8. You'll have to run a clean install.

WHICH VERSION IS FOR YOU?

Professional

Although an employer will handle buying Windows 8 licences in a big business, for a smaller office kitting out a few PCs or for people who work from home, **Windows 8 Pro** is the one to go for. You can upgrade to it directly from Windows 7 Professional or Ultimate without losing your files, and it includes the BitLocker security feature and file encryption, so you can be confident that vital company data won't end up in the wrong hands. Better still, Pro adds virtualisation options, and the ability to host a remote desktop session, so you can show your screen to colleagues in another office as you work.

Student

Although Windows 8 will meet a student's needs, their circumstances – often on the move, requiring work as well as play – is perhaps better suited to a **Windows RT** tablet. Similar to an iPad, they run apps and can be carried around with ease, but they do something the iPad doesn't: roll out the often-bundled portable keyboard and they're work laptops too, complete with Microsoft Office.

Family

Whether it's for the family unit as a whole, or for each of the individuals within it, the standard version of **Windows 8** includes all the essentials you need. You get the new Start screen and all the new Windows Store apps, including Internet Explorer 10 for browsing the web and Windows Defender to keep you protected. You can set up a different account for each family member, with picture passwords to make it even easier to make sure everyone can get to work. Windows 8 can be installed on everything from a powerful PC or a portable laptop right down to the new breed of Windows 8 tablets.

FAQ

Q: I've seen Windows 8 on sale with the letter "N" after the name of the edition. What does this mean?

A: The "N" editions of Windows 8 exist to satisfy certain legal requirements. They don't include Windows Media Player, yet they cost the same as regular editions. It's unlikely you'll see them in shops, but if you do they're best avoided.

for System Builder: despite the rather convoluted name this is essentially a fresh installation copy of Windows 8 for use on your own PC or laptop.

Whether you're looking to upgrade an existing system or install Windows 8 afresh, there are several ways to go about buying it. You can pick up a copy from many high-street retailers, but with broadband speeds generally a lot higher than when Windows 7 came out, the easier option is simply to download it directly from Microsoft's website.

UPGRADE VERSIONS Windows 8 may have been designed specifically with upgrade users in mind, but you'll still need to pick the right version in order to keep your existing files and applications intact when upgrading.

The standard Windows 8 can be installed over the top of Windows 7 Starter, Home Basic and Home Premium, which will cover most devices used in a home environment. However, if you happen to be running Windows 7 Professional or Ultimate, you'll be able to keep your installed applications only if you upgrade specifically to Windows 8 Pro.

For owners of PCs and laptops running Windows Vista or XP, you can still upgrade directly to either version of Windows 8 and keep your personal files intact, but you will lose any applications installed on your system. Make sure you have any necessary installation discs, or make a note of any applications you'll want to download and install again when your upgrade is complete.

WINDOWS RT There's one remaining version of Windows 8 for us to introduce, and it needs to be addressed separately as it's entirely new and is a different proposition to Windows 8 and Windows 8 Pro when it comes to the potential for upgrading and installing it yourself. It's called Windows RT, and it's the version of Microsoft's new operating system designed primarily for use on tablet devices.

Why is there a need for a dedicated tablet version of Windows? First, the portable nature of tablets means they favour a different type of processor to the x86-based processors you'll typically find in your standard laptop or PC. Most are designed by a company called ARM, and are specifically built to be more power-efficient so as not to drag down battery life. Windows RT is designed with that different architecture in mind, and is less demanding on system resources than the other variants of Microsoft's new operating system.

In addition, the touchscreen nature of tablets means you interact with them differently from the ground up. So while at its core Windows RT is largely the same as Windows 8, it comes with special touch-enhanced versions of Word, Excel, PowerPoint and OneNote built specifically for tablet use. You can't install normal desktop applications on a Windows RT device, you're limited to those specifically created for Windows RT in Microsoft's app store.

So why don't we need to talk about upgrades with Windows RT? Because quite simply the only way you can get it is pre-installed on a new tablet. You can't buy it separately, and you can't install it yourself on a PC or laptop. It's essentially Windows 8 Tablet Edition.

EDITIONS COMPARED

	Windows 8	Windows 8 Pro	Windows RT
Upgrade price	N/A	£24.99	N/A
Upgrades from Windows 7 Starter, Home Basic, Home Premium	●	●	·
Upgrades from Windows 7 Professional, Ultimate	·	●	·
USER INTERFACE			
Desktop	●	●	●
Start screen	●	●	●
Semantic Zoom	●	●	●
Live Tiles	●	●	●
Snap	●	●	●
Touch and Thumb keyboard	●	●	●
BUNDLED APPLICATIONS AND SERVICES			
Windows Store	●	●	●
Microsoft account	●	●	●
Windows Update	●	●	●
Apps (Mail, Calendar, People, Messaging, Photos, SkyDrive, Reader, Music, Video)	●	●	●
Internet Explorer 10	●	●	●
Updated Windows Explorer	●	●	●
Enhanced Task Manager	●	●	●
Windows Media Player	●	●	·
Installation of x86/64 desktop software	●	●	·
Microsoft Office (Word, Excel, PowerPoint, OneNote)	·	·	●
SECURITY AND BACKUP			
Windows Defender	●	●	●
File history	●	●	●
Picture password	●	●	●
Reset and refresh your PC	●	●	●
Trusted boot	●	●	●
BitLocker and BitLocker To Go	·	●	·
Encrypting File System	·	●	·
Device encryption	·	·	●
ADVANCED FEATURES			
Connected standby	●	●	●
SmartScreen	●	●	●
Switch languages on the fly	●	●	●
Better multiple monitor support	●	●	●
Storage Spaces	●	●	·
Exchange ActiveSync	●	●	●
ISO/VHD mount	●	●	●
Mobile broadband features	●	●	●
Play To	●	●	●
Remote Desktop (client)	●	●	●
VPN client	●	●	●
Boot from VHD	·	●	·
Client Hyper-V	·	●	·
Domain Join	·	●	·
Group Policy	·	●	·
Remote Desktop (host)	·	●	·

INSTALLING WINDOWS ON AN EXISTING PC OR LAPTOP IS EASIER THAN EVER, AND YOU SHOULDN'T LOSE ANY FILES AND APPLICATIONS ALONG THE WAY

Upgrading from Windows 7

Tip

If your PC or laptop is running an older version of Windows, you can still upgrade to Windows 8. While your vital files and folders will be retained, you won't be able to keep any applications installed. The first time you boot into Windows 8 you'll have to start from scratch, so make sure you have any installation discs and licence codes to hand.

Most consumer PCs and laptops are already running Windows 7, and Microsoft has done everything it can to make sure the transition to Windows 8 is as smooth as possible. In fact, the upgrade version is now the primary way to purchase the new operating system.

You can upgrade from any version of Windows 7, but the version you're running does affect which version of Windows 8 fits best – we cover the different editions and what they offer on p14. To sum up, though, if you're running Windows 7 Starter, Home Basic and Home Premium, you'll want to pick up the standard Windows 8. If you're running Windows 7 Professional or Ultimate, you should go for Windows 8 Pro.

You don't have to follow those rules, however. If you're prepared to install from scratch and lose your files and applications (with a good backup you can easily get the former back once you're up and running), you can choose whichever version of Windows 8 has the features you need. But for the least stressful installation it's best to match the versions correctly.

We're a long way past the old days of complex installers, multiple restarts, hours of updating and uncertainty over the result. Today it should be a case of setting the Windows 8 installation on its way, choosing a few settings and making a cup of tea. You'll only be asked to interact with the installation near the end, and even on an older machine the whole process should take no more than half an hour to complete – less on a new system.

If you have a physical disc, you can start the process by inserting it into the drive and rebooting. But it's much easier to insert the disc while already in Windows 7 and following the instructions from there. If you're installing a downloaded version, you'll start the whole process online. Just follow the instructions you were given at the time.

Say goodbye to the Windows desktop as you know it.

HOW TO...
INSTALL WINDOWS 8

① **BACK UP ANY VITAL FILES** It's extremely unlikely anything will go wrong with a simple upgrade from Windows 7, but if you have files on your PC or laptop that you absolutely can't live without – maybe some financial documents, a big music collection, or your masterpiece novel, for instance – save them to an external disk, or upload them to a service such as SkyDrive to make sure you can get them back if the worst does happen.

If you've knowingly chosen to upgrade to the "wrong" version of Windows 8 – one that won't let you keep your installed applications – make a list of the software you use, and either have the original installation discs to hand when upgrading, or see if they're available for free online.

② **START THE INSTALLER** The first thing you'll be asked to do once the installer starts is to check online for the latest updates. You don't have to do this right now – you can run Windows Update at any point once you're up and running – but going through the process now will save you hassle later on. However, if you don't want to, or haven't got the internet set up, just skip this step.

Depending on how you've bought Windows 8 and what media you're using to perform the install, the specifics of the next few steps may vary slightly. You may initially be asked to select your language, time zone and keyboard style – if so, make sure you choose UK English rather than US English, as it will save you many annoyances down the line. However, the installer may pick this up automatically, so don't be concerned if your computer skips this step.

You may also be prompted to get the final installation under way by clicking an Install Now button. Take note of the small "Repair your computer" option at the bottom of this screen – if anything should go wrong with your system in the future, this is a useful tool to get things working.

③ **ACTIVATE** Before you go any further, Microsoft wants to check that you've paid for your copy of Windows 8 and that it's a legal version. This involves entering your 25-character Windows 8 product key, which can be found either on the disc packaging if you bought it in the shops, or in your confirmation email if you bought online.

④ **START THE INSTALLER** Just type in the numbers and letters of the product key as you see them, the dashes will be added automatically. If your keyboard doesn't work in the installer for some reason, don't despair – simply click the keyboard button and an on-screen keyboard alternative will pop up instead, allowing you to select letters and numbers using the mouse instead of typing them out. Either way, as long as your copy of Windows 8 is legitimate, you should breeze through to the next screen.

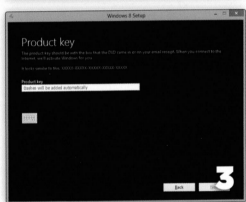
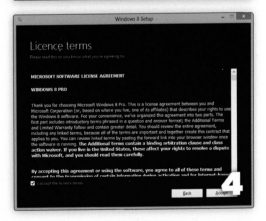

HOW LONG?
No more than 30 minutes; faster on a recent PC.

HOW HARD?
Very easy. The whole process is automated.

Q: I'm already running one of the pre-release versions of Windows 8. Can I upgrade to the final version?

A: You may be able to upgrade from the Consumer or Release Preview versions, but you won't be able to keep your applications in place. Make sure you back up everything before you start the installation process.

⑤ AGREEMENT The next screen you're faced with looks pretty complex – it's the exceedingly long licence agreement which covers your use of Windows 8. While the terms of this agreement are legally binding, no one will blame you if you don't read it. The main thing to be aware of is that your copy of Windows 8 is generally for one PC only. By ticking the box here, you're agreeing that you won't try to install it on other systems. That's standard fare.

⑥ TYPE OF INSTALLATION Next up is an important screen: the choice between simply going ahead with the default Upgrade procedure, or to choose a Custom installation. This screen will only appear if you buy particular versions of Windows 8. The default option attempts to keep all of your current files and settings in place. The second possibility, Custom, means you're opting for a clean install of Windows 8. This will wipe your system and start afresh, so think carefully before choosing it. We'll assume you're choosing to upgrade.

If that doesn't appear, you should move on to a preparation screen, which will check that you have everything you need and finalise the installation type you're going for. It will come back with several options: most people will want to tick the "Keep Windows settings, personal files and applications" option, although it's up to you.

⑦ CUP OF TEA That's the difficult part over with. From here the installer will spend some time copying the files across to your PC, unpacking them and then putting them in the right places. This may take anything from ten minutes to over half an hour depending on your system, but it doesn't require any input from you so feel free to leave it to its own devices. Also, don't worry if your system reboots at any point during the installation – that's normal, and you'll know when it's ready for your input again.

⑧ PERSONALISE It's at this point that you'll start to see the differences in Windows 8's look and feel. Your first step is to choose your colour scheme. There's a fair bit of scope for personalisation too – you can choose to stick to your favourite colour on dark grey if you like, or perhaps you'd prefer something a little louder or more outlandish. Do bear in mind, though, that whatever you end up going for will be the colour scheme you'll see every time you open the Start screen, so we'd advise restraint: don't choose bright pink unless you really are prepared to see it every day! That said, you can change your colour scheme at any time, so there's no need to get too bogged down by the details at this stage of the game. Once you're satisfied with your personalised colour scheme, turn your attention to the text box below

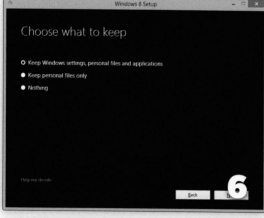

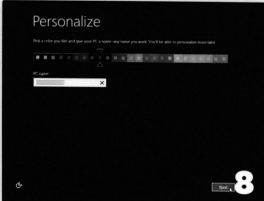

and give your PC a name. It's your choice, obviously, but we'd advise going for something you'll recognise if it appears on your home network – Jon's PC or Sarah's laptop, for example.

(9) **SETTINGS** At this point you may be given the option to join a wireless network – see p96 for more details. Otherwise, the next screen you'll see is the Settings page: it gives you two options covering automatic updates, privacy options and network sharing settings. You can either let Windows choose the default options and skip ahead several steps, or you can specify them yourself. For most people the default option should be fine, but be aware you may be allowing Microsoft and third parties to access some of your information via apps and the like. To be totally happy you know exactly what Windows 8 can and can't do, click Customize. This will take you through several further screens where you can toggle options on and off as required.

(10) **SIGN IN** We're almost done now, but this step may confuse Windows 7 users, as Windows 8 uses accounts in a different way. To make it easier to buy apps and sync devices, Windows 8 lets you sign in with your Microsoft account, which can have credit card information attached, and it can be used

across SkyDrive and several other services. For ease of use Microsoft wants you to create this account now (or sign in with it if you already have one). This is fine if you're okay logging in to this account every time you log on to your PC. But you don't have to: if it all sounds too inconvenient or insecure for your liking, you can choose to sidestep the process by clicking "Sign in without a Microsoft account".

(11) **SECURITY** Once you've entered your account password (if you have one), you may now be asked for additional information to bolster Windows 8's security still further, such as a phone number or an alternative email address to send reset options to should you forget your details or find yourself locked out of your PC. Again, none of this is compulsory. Next you'll be treated to a short "tutorial" on mouse gestures.

(12) **ENJOY WINDOWS 8** And that's it. After some final preparations, you should be presented with the new – and quite possibly unfamiliar or even daunting – Windows 8 Start screen. We'd advise familiarising yourself with the bundled apps, and navigating from apps to the desktop and back. Also, take a look at the options for fine-tuning the look and feel of the Start screen through extra icons and groups. It's all yours to do with as you will. Now that you've managed to get Windows 8 up and running, the rest of this book will take you through the features you're about to experience.

Tip

Windows 8 has drivers built in for most components and peripherals, so you shouldn't experience the pain of having to trawl the internet to get your USB ports working. If anything doesn't work, your first port of call should always be Windows Update, and then the manufacturer's website. Look for a Downloads or Support area, as this is where drivers are usually hosted.

THERE'S A NEW VERSION OF WINDOWS DESIGNED SPECIFICALLY FOR TABLETS, WITH A FEW KEY DIFFERENCES

Windows RT vs Windows 8

Although Microsoft has greatly simplified the range of Windows 8 editions, one option you may still be confused by is Windows RT. This is the version designed specifically for use on tablets – you won't be able to buy it or install it on a PC or a laptop.

Windows RT exists to surmount one major technical barrier with tablets. While laptops and PCs powered by Intel and AMD processors use something called the x86 architecture, tablets mainly use ARM processors. The two types are incompatible, and software written to run on one won't work on the other.

Almost all of the software we use on our computers today is made for x86 systems, which unfortunately means none of it will work on the current crop of ARM-based tablets. To get around this, Microsoft has produced a separate version of Windows that's built to run on ARM devices, and Windows RT is it.

A DIFFERENT APPROACH In practice this means some features you're used to might not be present on a Windows RT tablet. The main change is that while you can still access the desktop and browse your files and folders like on a normal PC, you won't be able to install normal Windows software. You can't just download the desktop version of

Google Chrome and set it up, for example, or grab the latest version of your favourite Twitter client.

Instead, all the software you run must come through the Windows Store. Developers can make both Windows 8 and Windows RT versions of their apps, and most of the apps in the Store should run across all versions of Windows. You should be able to get well-known software – there'll be app versions of the major browsers, for example – but if there's no app version of your favourite software in the Store, you won't be able to get it from elsewhere.

THE OFFICE EXCEPTION The one piece of software that circumvents this rule is Microsoft Office, and the good news is that every Windows RT tablet will come with a cut-down Office 2013 suite already installed. Microsoft has coded special Windows RT versions of Word, Excel, PowerPoint and OneNote to work on tablets, complete with touch-related enhancements to the interface.

Office 2013 brings plenty of new features, with Word getting new templates and PDF editing, and Excel benefitting from some nifty new fill features and chart options. You can now keep your files in the cloud with SkyDrive and, best of all, it runs on the desktop and feels just like the full Office suite.

Tip

◢ We really must reiterate the fact that Windows RT devices will not run standard desktop applications. Don't be fooled if you're shown the traditional desktop on a tablet in a shop – it's still there, but it's only there for handling your files. All applications must come from the Windows 8 Store. The training of salespeople can vary wildly, so go forearmed with this knowledge and don't let anyone persuade you otherwise.

Every Windows RT tablet will come with a basic version of Office 2013 pre-installed, with new features including a number of new Word templates.

Microsoft's own
Surface tablet will
be available in both
Windows 8 and
Windows RT variants

TWO KINDS OF TABLET All this Windows RT stuff sounds reasonably simple, right? It's just the tablet version of Windows 8. Except there's one other bit we haven't mentioned yet, and it complicates things somewhat: there are also more powerful x86 tablets that run Windows 8 rather than Windows RT.

Technologically, an ARM chip has some advantages over an x86 chip. ARM chips are generally low-power, energy-efficient components, designed for

More powerful
x86-based
Windows 8 tablets
will offer a more
traditional PC-like
experience

smaller devices such as smartphones. Their efficiency means Windows RT tablets should have longer battery life than their x86-based counterparts.

On the flipside, while an x86 chip may be more battery hungry, it's also likely to be a lot more powerful. So Windows 8 tablets won't last as long away from the mains, but they'll be much more capable of running demanding applications and performing complex tasks.

WHAT TO LOOK FOR If you look at Microsoft's own Surface tablets as an example, you'll see that there's a cheaper Surface with Windows RT and a more expensive Surface with Windows 8. The RT model has the limitations we've mentioned above, whereas the Windows 8 model has all the features you'd expect from a regular laptop or PC.

The distinction between the various versions of Windows allows manufacturers to create many different kinds of tablet – some cheap and built for content consumption, others powerful enough to be versatile working companions, and maybe even devices suitable for business use.

Perhaps the easiest way to think of it is that Windows RT is Microsoft's equivalent of iOS on the iPad, while Windows 8 remains the equivalent of OS X on Mac computers. One is designed purely for the use of apps, while the other can run the full-blown desktop software we've been running on our computers for years.

Tablets with Windows RT installed are therefore going to mainly be consumer products at much lower prices than their more serious Windows 8 cousins, but both versions have their unique appeal.

Tip

If you're unsure which version of Windows 8 a tablet is running, go to the Start screen, type "system" and click the Settings tab on the search results page. Tap the System option and a window will open on the desktop to tell you what version is installed.

Tip

Be careful to buy the
kind of tablet that
best suits your needs.
As we saw on the
previous page, there
are two different
types – Windows 8
and Windows RT – and
at this early stage it's
hard to know how
clearly the two types
will be advertised by
manufacturers and
retailers. If there's no
obvious branding to say
which type of Windows
a tablet uses, be sure
to ask before you
make a purchase.

⊙ Eight reasons to buy a Windows 8 tablet

The Apple iPad may be the current tablet king, but an exciting new wave of
Windows tablets has arrived to challenge it – and Windows offers tablet users
plenty that you simply can't get elsewhere. Not sure whether there's space in
your life for a Windows tablet? Here are eight reasons why it will be money
well spent

1 **IT'S MORE THAN JUST A TABLET** A tablet running
Windows 8 is not just a tablet – it's also a PC. The
presence of the traditional desktop, and the access to all
the tools, files and folders that brings, makes a Windows
tablet tremendously versatile. Whereas an iPad can only
run apps, a Windows 8 tablet can run any of your existing
Windows applications too. A Windows RT tablet isn't quite
so versatile, but it compensates with its bundled Office apps.

2 **GROUND-BREAKING DESIGNS** Unlike the Apple iPad,
which has dominated the tablet market for the past
few years, almost all of the first wave of Windows 8-based
tablets offer something on top of just the basic tablet form
factor itself. Most also incorporate a hardware keyboard in
some way, whether it's in the form of a docking station that
turns the tablet into a laptop, or a form factor that sees the
keyboard permanently attached but able to swivel out of
sight in an ingenious way.

3 **CONSISTENCY** Being Windows-based, there's not too
much to learn, so if you're running Windows 7 you
should be up to speed in Windows 8 in no time. Better still,
much like the relationship between the iPhone and the iPad,
a Windows 8 tablet has much in common with Windows
Phone 8, so if you buy one of the latest handsets from Nokia
or the many other brands making Windows Phones, you'll
be able to share information and even apps across your
different devices.

4 **APPS** Windows 8 tablets will run the Windows Store,
Microsoft's equivalent to the Apple App Store. You get
some excellent bundled apps pre-installed, but the Store will
have thousands more. On a tablet it's much easier to use an
app than a website, as they are specifically designed to make
the most of the tablet screen and interface. Look for your
favourite names and you're sure to find some apps to make
your life easier.

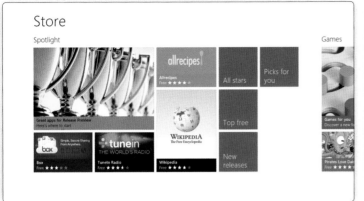

The new wave of Windows tablets boast all the familiarity of Windows but with an interface that's optimised for touch. The Windows Store has thousands of apps available to download, while with a SkyDrive account you can back up and share your own files with ease.

5 **LIVE TILES** The new touch-focused interface might not be ideally suited to a PC with a mouse and keyboard, but it's perfect for a tablet. The live tiles provide you with oodles of information right there on the Start screen, so you don't even need to open an app to see the latest news, weather and even your latest messages. Even the Lock screen can be set up to give you your favourite information without even unlocking the device.

6 **PERFORMANCE** Tablets running Windows 8 can be built upon the same internals as the average laptop. This means they're powerful – very powerful. Unlike an iPad, a Windows 8 Pro tablet will be able to do some intensive tasks, such as editing HD video and running applications such as Photoshop. Try doing more than the basics on other tablets and they'll grind to a halt; on a Windows tablet they're just as smooth as if you were running them on a full-blown PC or laptop.

7 **SKYDRIVE** Even the cheapest of Windows 8 tablets gets access to Microsoft's cloud storage facility, and there's an excellent app to make handling your files a breeze. Any files can be saved into your SkyDrive, which is linked to your Microsoft account. The files are still saved on the tablet itself, but also uploaded to this online locker. To access a file elsewhere, just log in to your SkyDrive and it will be there. It's ideal for keeping files safely backed up, or sharing them between computers.

8 **ACCESSORIES** Microsoft has produced some superb keyboards and mice to expand the capabilities of your Windows tablet. The Wedge Keyboard includes a case that hinges to turn into a handy tablet stand, while the mice have touch surfaces that support all of Windows 8's intuitive gestures. Pack a set in your bag and you have everything you need to work at home or on the move. You can even use your existing Windows 7 accessories.

IN THIS CHAPTER

28 **How the new Start screen works**
Find your way around the new Windows Start screen with our annotated guide.

30 **Discovering the Settings menu**
Navigate the all-new Settings section with our guide to its categories and options.

32 **The Windows 8 start screen**
Take an in-depth look at the big changes to the desktop experience in Windows 8.

34 **Introducing Charms and search**
Explore the Windows 8 Charms bar, which puts a wealth of common options at your fingertips.

36 **Personalising Windows 8**
Change colours, themes and the Lock screen's functions with our guide to Windows 8 personalisation.

38 **Setting up User Accounts**
Create and manage individual accounts for everyone who uses your PC.

40 **Introducing picture passwords**
Don't worry about forgetting a password: log on with pictures and gestures on your PC or tablet.

2
Introducing Modern UI

YOUR NEW-LOO

Microsoft has pushed the desktop to the background in Windows 8, introducing a new Start screen designed to be used across PCs, laptops and tablets. This full-screen interface is built around large, bright tiles that serve as gateways to your applications and folders. Some are even alive with information, dynamically updating themselves with the latest news headlines,

K WINDOWS

weather information and notifications from your email accounts. The radically redesigned Start screen has its own settings menus, search options and even a new toolbar, dubbed the Charms bar. We cover them all in this section, plus we look at how to personalise the Start screen – from changing its colour scheme to creating your own live tiles.

2
Introducing Modern UI

OUR ANNOTATED GUIDE TO THE NEW-LOOK WINDOWS 8 START SCREEN WILL HELP YOU FIND YOUR WAY AROUND THE OPERATING SYSTEM

How the new Start screen works

1 The **main Modern UI Start screen** is a living desktop composed of a mesh of interactive tiles. These not only launch the relevant applications – both Modern UI apps and traditional desktop software – but can also display snippets of data themselves, such as upcoming appointments, new emails and the latest headlines. The depth of tile stacks increases on larger screens, but the new interface introduces a lot of side-scrolling for the first time, which is hardly intuitive when using a keyboard and mouse.

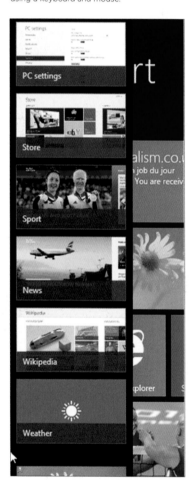

2 Move your finger to the left edge of the screen and quickly swipe your finger right and then left, or move your mouse to the left-hand corners of the screen and drag up or down, and you're presented with a strip of **thumbnails** showing a live preview of recently opened applications, so you can see at a glance what state they're in without opening them in full.

3 The design of the **Windows Store** echoes that of the new-look Windows Start screen, with apps tessellated together into categories such as Games or Music. The Store houses both Modern UI-style and traditional desktop apps, and developers have the opportunity to offer time-limited trials to showcase their wares.

4 Right-click on an ap tile (or hold down your finger) to activate ar **option menu** enabling you to unpin, uninstall or turn off live data for an app. This menu also houses the option to make tiles larger or smaller, although note that only full-width tiles can display live data. Right-click anywhere on the background to see an option to open a full list o apps that are installed on your system.

Tip

If you're not used to touch controls, don't panic – Windows 8 includes a short tutorial that can be viewed when the operating system is first installed, and it's designed to demonstrate some of the basic gestures that you'll need in order to navigate the Windows 8 Start screen.

10 To **personalise the Modern UI**, click the Settings charm and open the first menu in the Settings screen. Options you can adjust include your profile photo, background colours and patterns, and the photo used on the new Lock screen (which activates automatically after a set time, or manually by pressing Windows and L when on the Start screen).

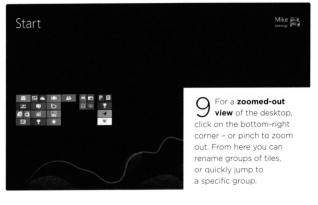

9 For a **zoomed-out view** of the desktop, click on the bottom-right corner – or pinch to zoom out. From here you can rename groups of tiles, or quickly jump to a specific group.

8 The horribly named **Charms** are activated by sending the mouse to the right-hand corners of the screen, by swiping in from the right-hand side of the screen on touchscreen devices, or by pressing Windows and C together. They include options to search, share data from apps, check the status of your connected devices, or twiddle with your PC's settings.

7 The **Search charm** allows you to search within individual Modern UI apps installed on your PC. By default, it's set to search for apps, settings and files – you can also do this by simply starting to type on the Start screen. However, click Store, for example, and you can search for apps in Microsoft's market, click Music to search for individual tracks or albums, and so on.

6 The **Settings charm** contains options to switch the notifications in the top-right corner of the Start screen on and off, manage your network connections and adjust speaker volume. It's here where you access the main Start screen settings menu and, somewhat oddly, it's also where you go to switch off and restart your PC.

5 The traditional **Windows desktop** is still there in Windows 8, and can be accessed via its tile or by pressing Windows and D together. Controversially, the Start button has been replaced by a blank [g]p, which you can left-click to go back to the Start screen or right-click [fo]r advanced options. The old Start menu, however, is no more.

Discovering the Settings menu

1 To open the **PC settings menu**, hover the mouse in the right-hand corners of the screen, open the Charms menu and click the Settings charm – or simply flick in from the right-hand side of the screen to open this menu on a tablet. Select Change PC settings to unlock the options available in the Modern interface. Note that this isn't the full range of settings available to the PC, just the most common ones – the traditional Control Panel is located on the Start screen and contains many of the options that more advanced users will be familiar with. The Modern UI's PC settings menu is easy to navigate: sections are listed on the left-hand side of the screen, and clicking on each of these titles will open up menus containing any relevant settings that can be adjusted on the right-hand side of the screen.

2 The **General tab** provides access to a range of basic PC options. You can configure the clock, activate or deactivate daylight savings time, turn app switching on and off, and adjust language and spelling options, including settings to have misspelt words automatically corrected or highlighted by Windows. This is also where to go to see how much storage space is available, which is handy if your PC or laptop has a small hard disk. Particularly useful is the option to refresh your PC – this leaves files, folders and applications in place, but clears out the other clutter that accumulates through everyday PC use.

PC settings

Personalise
Users
Notifications
Search
Share
General
Privacy
Devices
Wireless
Ease of Access
Sync your settings
HomeGroup
Windows Update

3 At the top of the Settings list is the **Personalise menu.** This enables you to customise the picture and applications used on the Lock screen, the colour and tattoo combinations used on the Start screen and its background, and the picture associated with your account. We've gone into more detail about personalising the Start screen on p36, but generally speaking, more detailed personalisation options can be found in the main Control Panel.

4 The **Users menu** gives the Administrator a variety of options relating to user accounts and how they can be accessed. The sign-in method can be switched between a password, PIN number or picture password (see p40 for more on this), and you can add additional local accounts for other users. You can also set whether logging in should require a Microsoft account, or with just a local account, and you can specify whether other users require a password to access their account.

Tip

This menu gives access to many of the more common options that will be used when it comes to personalising, securing and managing your PC, but more options are available elsewhere. The traditional Control Panel is available, and can be viewed when using the desktop interface.

9 Microsoft's **HomeGroup module** provides the most common
options for connecting to and sharing files with other
computers. If Windows 8 detects a HomeGroup it will be made
available for you to join, and sliding switches can be used to control
whether documents, music, printers, videos and pictures are shared
with other devices in the HomeGroup. Another switch allows TVs
and games consoles to play shared content, and a box at the
bottom of this menu will generate a unique code to allow others
to join the HomeGroup securely.

art screen   Account picture

ps

e background and show quick status and notifications, even when

detailed status

8 The **Ease of Access menu** provides options for making
Windows 8 simpler to use for those who need additional
help using the OS. One of Microsoft's familiar sliders can turn
the high contrast mode on or off, and another is used to make
text larger if your monitor supports it. Pressing Windows and
the up arrow key provides access to further accessibility tools,
from the magnifier and narrator to the on-screen keyboard,
and notifications can be set to stay onscreen for anything from
five seconds to five minutes. Cursor thickness can be changed,
too, should you wish to make it easier to see.

7 Windows 8's **Search menu** hunts
through apps, files and settings
by default, but the Search settings
offer more advanced options. Your
searches can be saved for future
reference, for instance, and apps that
you frequently search for displayed at
the top of the list, while there is also
a button to delete your entire search
history. A list of all installed Modern UI
apps can be accessed here, too, and
you can even specify individual apps
you wish to be omitted from searches
if you so choose.

5 The **Notifications area** includes options to turn app
notifications on or off globally, but relevant apps are also
listed individually with a slider next to each one, allowing you to
configure exactly which applications are able to alert you on the
Start and Lock screens. Most of Microsoft's pre-installed Modern UI
applications are listed here, as are some third-party applications –
the eBay and Amazon Kindle apps, for instance, are both integrated
into the notifications system.

6 The **Sync your settings** screen lets you customise which
options you want applied across all of your Windows 8
devices. You can fine-tune what exactly is synchronised too – from
desktop personalisation options and language preferences, to app
settings and browser options – and under what circumstances
it is synchronised. For example, Windows can be set to avoid
synchronisation over metered connections such as 3G, to avoid
chewing through masses of potentially expensive data.

The Windows 8 Start screen

Windows 8's Start screen is a far cry from the traditional desktop most users will be familiar with, and the switch to what Microsoft calls the Modern UI will certainly take some getting used to.

LIVE TILES The interface formerly known as Metro – now renamed Modern UI – replaces the traditional Start menu with a full-screen interface where applications, folders and drives are arranged in tiles: large, colourful icons that were first introduced in the Windows Phone 7 smartphone operating system.

Each tile represents one of the more prominent applications or services installed with Windows 8, at least initially. They're either square or rectangular, come in an array of colours, and many have dynamic features that help them provide up-to-date information.

The News tile, for instance, scrolls through the latest headlines, and the Photos tile provides a mini slideshow of pictures stored on your device. The Email app alerts you to how many unread messages you've got, and the Weather tool displays meteorological conditions that can be customised to your location.

Tiles don't have to be used for this default selection of applications, however. They can be removed, made larger or smaller, and have their live functionality switched on or off. Tiles can also be used for individual folders or even entire hard disks. We've gone into more detail about customising live tiles, and the rest of the Start screen's personalisation options, on p37.

NAVIGATING THE START SCREEN Users of other Windows operating systems will be familiar with pressing the Windows key to reveal the Start menu. That has now been consigned to history, and pressing the Windows key now switches between the Start screen and your most recently used application. You can still right-click in the bottom-left corner – this opens up a menu of advanced options, including the Control Panel.

The Start screen scrolls as you add more icons, but if you were expecting it to move vertically, think again; in Windows 8, the Start screen scrolls horizontally. On a tablet, you swipe your finger to scroll the Start screen; with a mouse, hover your cursor at the bottom of the screen and a scroll bar appears. If your mouse has a scroll wheel, you can use that too.

Windows 8 also includes Semantic Zoom, which can be accessed by pinching on touchscreens or clicking the little minus sign in the bottom-right corner using a mouse. This lets you see all of your apps, and you can rename groups of tiles or jump to specific groups.

Moving your mouse to the bottom and top right-hand corners of the Start screen unveils the Charms menu, which contains options for searching, sharing, connecting to external devices and accessing Windows 8's Settings menu. On a tablet, Charms are accessed by sweeping your finger from the right. Right-clicking on the Start screen, or swiping upwards from the bottom on a tablet, brings up a one-button menu at the bottom of the screen: the option to open a screen with all of your apps.

Tip

 As usual, a host of keyboard shortcuts are available to help with Start screen navigation. The arrow keys can be used to skip around tiles, and the End and Home buttons jump between the first and last tiles.

The new-look Start screen introduces horizontal scrolling for browsing your tiles.

HOW TO...
GET STARTED WITH LIVE TILES

(1) EXPLORING LIVE TILES Many of Microsoft's Modern UI applications have their own live tiles, but they need prompting to start displaying relevant information. Click the Weather app, for instance, and choose Places. In this interface you can choose your default location, and only then will current weather conditions start appearing in the live tile. Many other apps, including the Finance, News and Sport apps, also need initial interaction before they start working fully.

(2) TWEAK YOUR LIVE TILES Some of the applications that push data to your live tiles can be edited to display different information. Open the Weather application again, head back to the Places menu, and enter a place name to find its weather. Then right-click on your new location on the main screen of the Weather app and choose to pin this different location to the Start screen. The Mail app can be customised in a similar way. While the live tile is set up to display messages from your inbox by default, you can set up additional live tiles to display information from other folders: simply right-click on the email account folder you'd like to use and click "Pin to Start". While most live tiles relate to pre-installed apps and services, a host of third-party applications have their own live tiles in place, although the degree of customisation and activity varies considerably. The Financial Times, Sky News and Wikipedia tiles all scroll through the latest stories and articles, for instance, while various travel apps show the latest rail or road conditions.

(3) MEASURE LIVE TILE PERFORMANCE Microsoft is keen to ensure that live tiles don't put a drain on either system performance or – in the case of laptops and tablets – battery life. To see for yourself just how much of its processing power your PC is using, head to the Start screen and type "task manager". Once you've opened the Task Manager, click the "App history" tab. This lists the applications you've used on your PC and how much processor and network resources each of them has accounted for. The final column, Tile updates, shows how much memory has been used up in keeping each tile's contents updated. If any are using significantly more than the rest, or more than you'd like, return to the Start screen – from here you can deactivate the tile and put a stop to it.

(4) TURN OFF TILES Deactivating or removing live tiles is simple, and useful if you'd like to customise your Start screen or cut down on the clutter that's inevitably going to start building over time. To remove tiles, head to the Start screen and right-click a tile you'd like to make changes to. Click the "Turn live tile off" button at the bottom of the screen to turn it back into a standard tile with a static icon. This will stop updates and notifications appearing on tiles and needlessly draining system resources. To remove a tile entirely and simplify your Start screen, right-click it and select "Unpin from Start" at the bottom of the screen. You can also right-click multiple tiles and remove them simultaneously if you'd like to make more sweeping changes to your Start screen.

HOW LONG?
There's plenty new here, from tiles to Charms, and it will take some time for even experienced users to become familiar with all the new features.

HOW HARD?
The wealth of new features on board Windows 8 means even experienced users could get caught out initially.

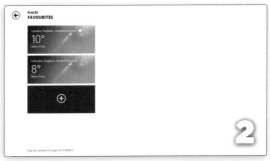

WINDOWS 8'S CHARMS GIVE EASY ACCESS TO KEY FEATURES, AND THEY'RE
ACCESSIBLE FROM BOTH THE START SCREEN AND THE DESKTOP

Introducing Charms and search

As well as introducing its controversial new Start screen in
Windows 8, Microsoft has added another new feature that
will doubtless also divide opinion: Charms.

These are icons housed in a universal toolbar that
pops up on the right-hand side of the screen, and they can
be accessed no matter where you are in the OS – using an
application, navigating the Start screen or using the desktop.
Opening the Charms menu is easy: either hover your cursor
over the top or bottom right-hand corners of the screen, or
swipe in from the right on a touchscreen.

SEARCH Sitting at the top of the menu is the Search
Charm, which you'll probably use the most. Click it, and the
Charms menu is replaced by the Search box on the right of
the screen. Searching is incredibly fast in Windows 8, and
results are no longer displayed immediately in a long list as
soon as they're found. Instead, results are divided into three
categories – Apps, Settings and Files – with each returning
their own filtered results. The numbers published to the
right of each category indicate exactly how many results
there are in each.

Clicking a category then presents a list of relevant
search results on the left-hand side of the screen. The Apps,
Settings and Files categories are searched by default, but
it's possible to search within Modern apps too. Any that
can be searched are listed in the right-hand panel below
the three default categories. Windows 8 can hunt through
plenty of apps out of the box: Bing, Internet Explorer,

Mail, Maps, Music and more, with results all displayed on
the left-hand side.

Note that you can also get to the Search menu
simply by typing search terms from the Start screen.

SHARING AND DEVICES The Share charm comes into its
own when using an application launched from the Start
screen. The specific options available vary, but typically
involve sending photos, documents or files to other people
or devices. In the Photos app, for instance, it's possible to
select multiple pictures and send them to others via email or
by uploading them to your SkyDrive.

Sharing options are available in the News, Sports
and Travel apps, too – navigate to a story or category you
want to share, open the Charms menu, and select the Share
charm. This can't be done on the desktop or on the Start
screen directly, however.

Open up the Devices charm and you'll see options
for connecting a second monitor. The options for adding
a dual screen have been expanded: the desktop can be
duplicated or extended onto a second screen, and you can
choose to use one but not the other. You can also have
different background images on each, though this can only
be done from the desktop's Control Panel.

Printers will also appear in the Devices charm's
menu if configured to allow Modern UI functionality, while
the Devices charm can also be used to send music and other
files to media players.

Tip

The Devices charm
doesn't just handle
second monitors – if
you've got a projector
or TV attached to your
system it will reveal
options for those, too.
Before connecting
a peripheral and
assuming it'll work,
though, make sure
that your drivers are
up to date – many
manufacturers may
release updated
drivers to ensure their
peripherals work fully
with Windows 8.

The Charms menu can
be accessed on the
right of the screen at
any time.

HOW TO...
USE THE SETTINGS CHARM AND CUSTOMISE SEARCH

① **OPEN THE SETTINGS CHARM** Hover your mouse in one of the right-hand corners of the screen and the Charms menu will pop up; tablet users simply swipe in from the right side of the screen. Click the bottom Charm, Settings, and the Charms menu will be replaced by the Settings panel. On the bottom are icons giving access to six of the most regularly used settings on any PC: a wireless networking indicator, volume and brightness controls, shortcuts to the notifications area and the on-screen keyboard, plus boot and restart settings.

② **TWEAK COMMON SETTINGS** Many of these settings will be familiar from Windows 7's Taskbar notification area, and they're just as easy to use. Clicking the Wireless icon, for instance, opens up a menu that illustrates all the wireless connections your PC can detect – click on them individually and you're able to connect to different sources. The Volume and Brightness icons open up sliders for you to make adjustments to sound and the screen, and clicking the Notifications box opens up any current notifications – and provides the option for you to set messages to remain hidden for one, three or eight hours. The Power button gives you three familiar options: Shut Down, Sleep and Restart.

③ **EXPLORE THE SETTINGS MENU** Underneath these six icons is the option "Change PC settings". This opens the Settings menu – at least as far as the Modern UI is concerned. It still isn't as in-depth as the main Control Panel, which can be found on the desktop and is largely unchanged from Windows 7, but you still have options for PC tweaking. User account options are found here, as are privacy, wireless and ease of access tools.

④ **CUSTOMISE THE SEARCH MENU** Scroll down the left-hand side of the Settings menu until you find the Search section. Here you're able to customise the results that can be accessed through the Charms menu's Search functionality. Windows lists the apps you use most often at the top of the list, and will change to reflect your usage habits. It also saves your searches to be used as suggestions in the future. However, both these options can be turned off. From here you can choose to delete your search history, but most of the window is dominated by a list of searchable Modern UI apps on your system. All are active by default, but with a click of its slider button an app can be prevented from appearing in search results – so if there's an app that's clogging up your search results, it's easy to deactivate.

HOW LONG?
Most Charms are straightforward, and only a couple have more complicated settings.

HOW HARD?
Charms are easy to access and, thanks to simplicity and their resemblance to Windows 7 options, are just as easy to use.

THE WINDOWS 8 START SCREEN LOOKS GREAT, BUT WITH THE CUSTOMISATION OPTIONS AVAILABLE IN WINDOWS 8 YOU CAN MAKE IT LOOK EVEN BETTER

Personalising Windows 8

Windows 8 is the most attractive operating system Microsoft has produced, so it's fitting that it's also relatively easy to customise. The process of tweaking the interface to match your own tastes and preferences starts before Windows is even installed – during the setup process, you're asked to pick which two-tone colour scheme you'd like to use throughout the OS.

COLOUR OPTIONS If you change your mind after installation, or want to further customise Windows 8's appearance, the Modern UI interface has several customisation options. To find these, you'll need to open the Charms menu, click the Settings charm, and open up the Change PC settings area. Personalisation options can be found in the first category.

If you don't like the colour combination you chose initially during the Windows 8 installation process, it's easy enough to make a change, and you're not short of options, either. Windows 8 offers a selection of 25 colours to choose from. These two-tone options will be manifest right across Microsoft's Modern UI interface, affecting the appearance of what Microsoft calls "tattoos", icons, taskbars, highlighted options and more.

The Personalise menu is where these so-called "tattoos" are to be found – there are 20 of them in all. These are the wallpapers that sit behind the Start screen's tiles and, while the selection can't be customised, the images on offer here span several artistic styles – so hopefully you'll find something you like.

CUSTOMISE THE LOCK SCREEN The Lock screen is the first thing you see when you turn on your PC, so it's well worth taking the time to tweak its appearance and functionality. Options to customise the Lock screen are, again, found in the Personalise area of the Start screen settings menu.

The first option lets you change the Lock screen background itself. Six images are included by default, including a Seattle skyline, an image of a piano, plus some abstract patterns, but the Browse button allows you to choose your own background image.

More interesting is the ability to set up to seven applications to always run in the background, even when the PC isn't in use, with any notifications or messages popping up on the Lock screen for your immediate attention. The instant messaging, email and calendar apps are chosen by default, and at the time of writing, the Weather app is the only option you can add manually when you first install Windows 8. Some third-party apps offer this functionality, though, and you have the potential for up to seven Lock screen applications in total.

One app can be chosen to display more detailed information, although by default the Weather and Calendar apps are the only options. The former will list your location's temperature and weather forecast on the Lock screen; the latter your next appointment.

The Personalise menu also gives you the option to change your User Account image. If your PC, laptop or tablet has a webcam, you can use it to take a new picture. Otherwise, you can browse your PC for a suitable image.

Tip

Don't be afraid to unpin tiles from the Start screen entirely. A wide variety of apps are included on the Windows 8 Start screen by default, but if you know you're not going to use certain ones, there's no sense in leaving them there. You can always open them by typing their name into Search.

Windows 8's Modern UI interface comes with a wide range of personalisation options accessible through the PC settings area. The 25-colour palette gives you control over the overall two-tone colour scheme, while background images, the Lock screen and your own User Account image can be adjusted here too.

HOW TO...
TWEAK YOUR TILES

 MOVE TILES Windows 8 has a respectable set of tiles enabled by default, and the Start screen enables you to personalise this part of the OS. Moving tiles around the screen is as simple as clicking a tile and dragging it to your desired new location. Other tiles slide out of the way, automatically moving to their new positions when the moved tile is dropped into place, even if you're moving tiles from one Start screen group to the next.

 CUSTOMISE TILES Right-clicking a tile brings up further customisation options at the bottom of the screen: live tile options can be turned off if they're irritating or chewing through too much power; tiles can be made larger or smaller – square tiles can be made rectangular, and vice versa; and tiles can also be removed entirely. This is handy if you have plenty of apps installed that are clogging up your Start screen.

 ADD NEW APPLICATION TILES Any app you install – either new Modern UI-style apps or old desktop apps – should install a tile onto the Windows 8 Start screen by default. But if you've removed a tile previously and decide you wish to reinstate it, there are a variety of ways you can go about it. If you know the name of the application you wish to restore, simply type its name when you're on the Start screen to launch a search. Assuming you've typed the name correctly it will pop up in the search results, in which case you can simply

right-click its icon and choose Pin to Start and its tile will be reinstated without any further ado.

If you're not sure of an application's name or don't have a specific app in mind, right-click anywhere on the Start screen's background to bring up the All Apps option at the bottom of the screen. This is also useful should you wish to restore multiple apps at a time: you can right-click several and choose the Pin to Start option to have them appear simultaneously on the Start screen.

ADD FOLDERS AND DRIVES AS TILES Tiles on the Windows 8 Start screen aren't restricted solely to applications. Folders containing important documents or pictures, for instance, can also be pinned to the Start screen to be more readily accessible. To add folders to the Start screen, head to the desktop, navigate to the folder you wish to pin using Windows Explorer, and right-click it. Click the Pin to Start option and it will appear on your Start screen as a new tile, and it can then be repositioned or resized as you see fit. External and network drives can also be given their own tiles – handy if you keep important data on an external hard disk or media on a NAS drive that the whole family uses, for instance. Adding these tiles to your Start screen is just as easy as adding local folders – simply navigate to their location on your PC using Windows Explorer, right-click the drive or folder, and select the Pin to Start option in the bar at the bottom of the screen. The tiles aren't as bright and colourful as the ones used for apps, however.

HOW LONG?
With so many customisation options available, it'll take a bit of time to get the new interface looking ship-shape.

HOW HARD?
There are plenty of options, but most of them are straightforward – even for beginners.

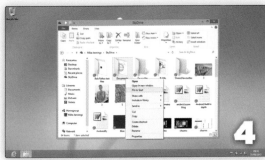

USER ACCOUNTS IMPROVE SECURITY, ALLOW FOR GREATER CONTROL OVER YOUR PC, AND GIVE EACH USER THEIR OWN PERSONAL SPACE

Setting up User Accounts

One of the most common security blunders on a family PC is for everyone to have access to the same Administrator account, potentially giving children the power to delete vital files or access private documents.

Even worse, it provides an open door for everyone to install their own software. So when the kids decide to load that tempting free game they found online that's actually a scam designed to steal your bank account details, you're left wide open to attack.

To help prevent younger (and even older) users running wild, Microsoft offers several security measures in Windows 8, with individual user accounts returning after proving a popular feature in Windows Vista and 7. Each person can have their own account, which is unlocked via a login password. This gives them access to all essential applications, files and documents, but limits access to features that could compromise the security and stability of your PC – or the Administrator's privacy.

It also means parents are able to apply separate parental controls for each child, preventing them from using the PC late at night, for example. See p116 for more on Windows 8's parental controls.

TYPES OF ACCOUNT Windows 8 now allows the use of Microsoft accounts for logging onto a PC, using your Microsoft email address as your username. Choosing this option brings with it several advantages, such as the synchronisation of settings, contacts and SkyDrive files across multiple devices.

Windows 7 offered administrator, local and guest accounts, and these options are largely untouched in Windows 8. The Administrator account is assigned to the first person who sets up the PC, whether with a Microsoft or local account. Administrator accounts have full control over the computer, with the ability to add new software and hardware, make changes to key settings, and set up and delete other user accounts.

On a family PC, it makes sense to have just one Administrator account, with everyone else using standard Microsoft or local accounts. They'll be able to access software already on the PC, create and delete files, personalise the desktop and Start screen and save their own browser bookmarks and toolbars – but won't be able to install software without an Administrator password.

You can fine-tune these settings to a certain degree, ranging from the Administrator being notified whenever any software is installed or any changes made, to these notifications being turned off altogether.

Finally, there's the Guest account, which is largely the same but is designed for visitors needing temporary access to a PC. This account isn't active by default – to switch it on, open up the Control Panel in the desktop, head to the Manage Accounts section, and click the Guest Account icon.

Tip

Head to the Settings menu in the Start screen, click the Users tab, and switch from a Microsoft account to a local account. This is useful if you'd like to make changes to your Microsoft account separately, but it does mean your settings won't sync between machines.

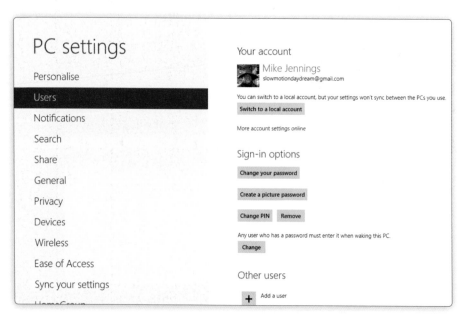

The Users section of the PC settings menu allows you to configure your own user account and add other users, but for complete control of user accounts you'll need to head to the full Control Panel on the desktop.

HOW TO...
SET UP USER ACCOUNTS

① CREATE A NEW ACCOUNT When you load Windows 8 for the first time, you'll be asked to create a new account. If you have already registered for a Microsoft account, enter its address and password and your data will then be synchronised within a few seconds. If you don't have a Microsoft account or just want a standard user account that isn't linked to it, you can choose that option. Be aware that you won't be able to enjoy features such as synchronised settings and one-click purchases from the Windows Store if you don't sign in with a Microsoft account. Choose a username and password along with a password hint should it slip your mind. Review this information on the next page and, if adding an account for a child, note the Family Safety tick box letting you monitor their PC usage.

② PASSWORD-PROTECT THE ACCOUNT Windows 8 offers several options to password-protect your account, including the ability to sign in with a picture password (see p40). To amend an existing password, go to the Users tab of the Settings screen, click "Change your password", and enter the new password you want assigned to the account. With Windows 8 you can also now log in using a four-digit PIN number rather than a password. To set this up, click Create a PIN in the Settings menu. You'll then be asked to enter your account's password – once that's done, enter your chosen four-digit code, type it in again to confirm, and click Finish.

③ MODIFY ACCOUNTS Only an Administrator is able to change account types, and only from the User Accounts section of the desktop's Control Panel. The Start screen's settings menu enables you to modify your own account, but you can't configure others. If you're an Administrator but want to downgrade to a standard account, for example, you'll have to appoint another Administrator first – Windows needs at least one user to be set up as an Administrator at all times. To change the status of another account, click the "Manage other accounts" link, select an account you'd like to change, and make your changes. The process is straightforward, with options to change the account's name, password, picture and type. To alter your own account, click the "Change your account type" link in the User Accounts section and you'll be presented with the same options.

④ DELETING ACCOUNTS Accounts can't be deleted from the more limited Options menu in the Start screen's settings area – this too involves a visit to the desktop Control Panel again. To delete an account, click its icon and choose the "Delete account" option. You'll be asked whether you wish to delete any of the documents or other files associated with the account too – note that if you do decide to keep them, they'll be stored in a folder on the desktop of the Administrator. Once you're happy with everything, press the Delete account button and the account in question will be no more.

HOW LONG?
Most people won't need to do much more than log in, but it'll take a little while longer for Administrators to set up their PC's accounts.

HOW HARD?
Administration options govern software installation and PC settings options, so don't tweak these unless you're sure of what you're doing.

Introducing picture passwords

Windows 8 lets you sign in with normal passwords and now PIN numbers too, but Microsoft has also introduced a third way to access your account – picture passwords.

WHAT IS A PICTURE PASSWORD? Microsoft has introduced picture passwords for several reasons, with ease of access a primary concern. Picture passwords have been designed to complement traditional text passwords, rather than replace them, and have been done so specifically with touchscreen devices in mind.

After all, while it makes sense to bolster your account security by choosing a password made up of complex strings of letters and numbers, having to enter that password by pecking away at a tablet's on-screen keyboard is an entirely different proposition to the relative ease of typing it out on a physical one.

The alternative, then, is to require specific touch gestures on top of an image of your choosing in order for an account to be accessed. These can be combined in any number of creative ways – your password could involve drawing a circle around a picture of your child's face, followed by a single press above, for instance.

Microsoft says picture passwords will improve security, as they're trickier to guess than text-based PINs or passwords. To prove the point, it has calculated that an eight-character alphabetical password has 208 billion unique combinations, while its multi-gesture picture passwords offer trillions of potential options.

The inherent strength of picture passwords themselves isn't the only security improvement either. If a picture password is entered incorrectly five times, you're prevented from trying again and will have to use your plain-text password instead. Picture passwords are disabled in remote and networked environments, too, to prevent network-based attacks.

HOW TO USE PICTURE PASSWORDS The option to create a picture password can be found in the Users menu of the Start screen's settings area – to get there, open the Charms menu by pointing your cursor at the right-hand corners of the screen, choose the Settings charm and click "Change PC settings". Enter your account's standard password when prompted.

Windows 8 lets you pick from any picture stored on your PC, in your Photos app or on your SkyDrive, and that gives you plenty of scope – the Photos application includes pictures from your Facebook and Flickr accounts, after all, as well as images from other systems on your network. Once you have chosen a picture, position it in the picture password pane then click "Use this picture". Now comes the all-important step of drawing your gestures. You can draw three using any combination of circles, straight lines and taps, but make sure you remember your movements – the gestures, their positioning on the image and the order in which they're made are all integral parts of the password.

HOW LONG?
Setting up a picture password is quick – the longest part of the process is picking a picture to use.

HOW HARD?
Microsoft's step-by-step instructions make the process easy, and the entire picture password system is designed for simplicity.

Tip

◣ The picture password configuration tool can only be accessed through the Start screen – there's no option to configure these when you're in the desktop mode and the Control Panel.

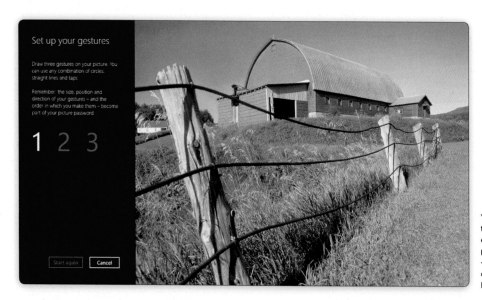

Set up your gestures

Draw three gestures on your picture. You can use any combination of circles, straight lines and taps.

Remember: the size, position and direction of your gestures – and the order in which you make them – become part of your picture password.

1 2 3

Start again   Cancel

You can include up to three gesture components in your picture password – any combination of circles, straight lines and taps.

Hosted technology,
minus the headaches

TODAY, TOMORROW & THE FUTURE

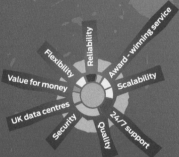

You're our priority
today, tomorrow and the future

Whether you're starting from scratch or a tech wizard, unreliable technology, limited product choice and a lack of support are all headaches you could do without.

Fasthosts has been delivering industry-leading technologies, for thousands of customers just like you for over 13 years. With wholly-owned and managed secure UK data centres, dedicated 24/7 support and a team of experts, Fasthosts are always here, supporting you every step of the way.

For help and advice call us now on **0800 6520 444**

WEB HOSTING · DOMAINS · EMAIL · DEDICATED SERVERS · VIRTUAL SERVERS · RESELLER HOSTING

IN THIS CHAPTER

44 Mail, People and Calendar

Find out how to juggle multiple email accounts, keep up to date with the latest developments on your social networks, and manage your diaries.

46 Music and Video

We explain how to enjoy the music and video stored on your home PCs, plus how to buy and rent movies and music from Microsoft's online stores.

48 Photos and Camera

Find out how to browse the photos stored on your PC and multiple social networks with the Photo app, and take new photos for the collection with Camera.

50 News, Sport, Finance and Travel

Set up tailored news channels, keep abreast of your team's latest results, manage your stock portfolio, and book a holiday with these four fantastic apps.

52 Bing Maps and Search

You'll never get lost – either in real life or on the web – with our guide to using the two Bing apps pre-installed on Windows 8.

54 Introducing the Windows Store

Find out how to hunt down, pay for and install thousands of new apps from the new Windows Store with our comprehensive guide.

56 20 of the best Modern apps

We root through the Windows Store to find 20 great apps to get you started on your new Windows 8 tablet, laptop or PC.

3
Modern apps

INTRODUCING M

Windows 8 introduces a whole new class of apps to the operating system. Previously known as "Metro style apps", but now merely referred to as Modern apps, these are more akin to the small, lightweight apps found on smartphones and rival tablets than the full-blown Windows apps of yesteryear. In this chapter, we'll introduce you to the Modern apps that come

ODERN APPS

pre-installed with Windows 8 and explain how to get the most from them. We'll also introduce you to the Windows Store, where you can find thousands more apps to download and install yourself. Finally, we'll pick our 20 favourite apps from the Windows Store to give you a flavour of what you can do with your new Windows 8 device.

3
Modern apps

 WINDOWS 8 INCLUDES A TRIO OF PRE-INSTALLED APPS THAT HELP KEEP YOUR LIFE IN ORDER. HERE WE EXPLAIN HOW TO GET THE MOST FROM THEM

Mail, People and Calendar

It's been a long while since Windows shipped with software for common, everyday tasks such as reading your email and managing your diary. Many of us may now use online services from companies such as Google, Yahoo and even Microsoft itself for webmail, storing our contacts and juggling our calendars. A trio of apps that are pre-installed on Windows 8 will save you from even having to open a web browser to access all of these functions.

MAIL The new Windows Mail application will be in prime position at the top left of the Windows Start screen the very first time you fire up Windows 8. If you've used your Microsoft Hotmail/Windows Live Mail account details as the login for your Windows 8 device, you should find that the Mail app has already downloaded the most recent messages from your Microsoft webmail account when you first click on the Mail tile.

Mail can be used to read and reply to messages from a variety of webmail and other email accounts. When you first open Mail, you should see a prompt to add another account in the bottom left-hand corner of the screen. If not, simply swipe in from the right-hand edge of the screen on a tablet, or hover your mouse in the bottom right-hand corner of the screen on a PC or laptop, to open the Settings charm from within the Mail app, and click on Accounts.

If you're adding another Hotmail, MSN, Windows Live, Outlook.com or Google Gmail account, all you have to do is select the relevant option and enter your username and password for that service. Mail will do the

rest, importing all your recent emails, folders and other settings. Mail can also access Microsoft Exchange accounts, which are typically used within businesses. Again, you may be able to set this up with nothing more than your email address and password, although you may be prompted for extra details, such as your email server and domain name. Your company's IT department should be able to provide you with these details, and you should check first that your IT manager is happy for you to download work email on a personal device. Some organisations may restrict access to work email for security reasons.

Once you've entered all your account details, you should find that you can switch between your different accounts by clicking on the green-coloured tabs in the bottom left-hand corner of the screen. The number next to each account name shows how many unread messages are waiting in that particular inbox.

To type a new email message, simply click the + button at the top of the screen. By default, Mail will send the message from the email address of the mailbox you're currently reading, but if you click on the little arrow next to your name in the top left-hand corner, you can change the account from which mail is sent. Mail will automatically fill the names and email addresses of contacts as you start typing them in the To or CC fields. Alternatively, you can click the little + sign next to each field and select mail recipients from within the People app (see below).

Subject lines are entered at the top of the screen, and you type your email message in the blank pane on the

Tip

If you don't want your emails or appointments appearing on your Windows 8 Start screen – to prevent inquisitive colleagues reading over your shoulder, for example – you can switch off live tiles. Simply press your finger or hold the left mouse button down on the Mail/Calendar tile for a second or two, then lift it gently upwards. At the foot of the screen you will see the option to turn the live tile off. You can switch it back on at any time.

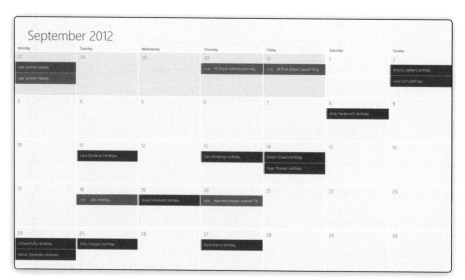

You can change the colours in the Calendar app if you don't like the defaults.

Top left: The Mail app automatically imports all your mail and contacts from your existing accounts.

Above: The People app collates all the latest updates from your social networks in a single place.

Left: Contacts in the People app include much more than simply an email address and a photo.

HOW LONG?
It takes only a few minutes to sign into your various accounts and import all your mail, contacts and calendar entries.

HOW HARD?
The hardest thing is remembering your passwords, although email setup is a little more complex for Exchange accounts.

right-hand side of the screen. At first sight, you may think you can do nothing more than type a plain text email in the default font, but drag your finger up from the foot of the screen on a tablet, or right-click on your mouse, and a set of new options will appear, including the abilities to change font, paste text or photos stored in the clipboard and attach a photo or document to the email.

Finally, Mail is one of the Windows 8 apps with live tile data. That means snippets of unread messages will scroll through the Mail tile on the Start screen, which is handy if you're waiting for a particular message to arrive.

PEOPLE People is a dual-purpose application. Not only does it store all your contacts, it also provides live updates from your social networks.

If you've set up webmail accounts in the Mail app, you should find that your email contacts have been automatically added to the People app. You can also pull in contacts from a range of social networks, including LinkedIn, Facebook and Twitter using the Accounts link in the top right-hand corner of the People app screen. Don't worry if you have the same contact stored in a number of different social networks; People does a good job of combining the data from the different social networks and listing all the email and Twitter addresses under a single contact card for that person.

If you're an avid Twitter/Facebook user, the What's New section of the People app is very useful. This collates all the updates from your various social networks into a single stream, so that you can see the latest tweets appearing from @StephenFry alongside the latest photos of your niece posted on Facebook.

People also lets you view your latest Notifications, so if someone's mentioned you in a Twitter message or tagged you in a photo on Facebook, you'll find out about it here. The People tile on the Start screen also displays the latest notifications, as well as photos of your friends.

CALENDAR If you've set up your Mail app to import your personal and work email, you should also find that your diaries have been synchronised in the Calendar app. The Calendar has day, week and month views that you can alter by swiping up from the bottom of the app screen or by clicking the right mouse button.

Each of your calendars are given their own colour code. If you don't like the default colour scheme, open Calendar's Settings charm by dragging in from the right of the screen or hovering the mouse in the bottom-right corner, then select Options and pick a different colour.

The Calendar's live tile displays forthcoming appointments on the Windows Start screen, which is handy for reminding you about meetings during the working day.

Music and Video

Tablets are designed for consuming content, and Microsoft has put the Music and Video apps front and centre in Windows 8. These two apps – which come pre-installed on the Windows 8 Start screen – are designed for playing back content stored on other PCs and drives on your network and the internet, as well as that on your device. With only a few clicks, you can buy or rent movies and music from Microsoft, and play the content back on a variety of devices, including a Windows smartphone or an Xbox console.

MUSIC When you first fire up the Windows 8 Music app, you should be presented with a neat stack of tiles showing the albums in your PC's music collection. Click on one of these tiles and you're presented with the options to play the entire album or add it to your "now playing" list, which allows you to create a playlist of songs that are queued up and ready to play on your machine. You can also select individual tracks to play or add to the queue.

You'll also see the option to Explore Artist, which pings you to an attractive homepage for the band or artist you're currently listening to. From here you can access a list of songs from that artist stored on your PC and their wider discography. Click on an album in the discography and you

can buy albums or individual tracks from the Microsoft Store. Irritatingly, music and video must be purchased using Microsoft's virtual currency, which makes it tricky to work out how much content actually costs: at the time of writing, 1,000 Microsoft points cost £8.50.

If you haven't already set up a Microsoft account, you can do so by opening the Settings charm from within the Music app. To do this, drag your finger in from the right-hand side on a tablet or hover the mouse in the bottom right corner on a PC, click on Account and fill in your details.

If you want to listen to music while you continue to browse other apps, you can drag the Music window to either side of the screen. You'll still be able to see what track is currently playing and access your playlists, but you'll also be able to play a game, browse the web or access any other Modern App installed on your system.

The music player has its own volume controls, but if you're playing music in the background and need to adjust the volume, the Windows volume controls are now found in the Settings charm; swipe your finger from the right of the screen or hover the mouse in the bottom right-hand corner of the screen to access them. Tablets will have their own volume control buttons.

Tip

Shop around for movie and music downloads before buying from the Windows Store. Online download stores such as Amazon.co.uk and film rental services such as LoveFilm and Netflix will often offer cheaper deals than Microsoft for the same music and movies. They will all play perfectly fine on Windows 8 PCs.

HOW TO...
BUY, RENT AND PLAY FILMS

① PLAYING YOUR VIDEOS When you first fire up the Video app, you'll see any movies stored on your device in My Videos. If you can't see a video you know is on your PC, flick up from the bottom of the screen or right-click on the mouse and select Open File. From there you can browse your PC and home network. If you've set up a Homegroup (see p94) and want to watch a video on your tablet that's stored on the PC in the bedroom, for example, click on the down arrow next to Files, select Homegroup and navigate to the video on your PC.

② BUY A MOVIE The Spotlight section of the Video app shows films available to buy or rent, while the Movies Store is divided into new releases, top-sellers and genres. If you can't find a movie by browsing, open the Search charm – by flicking from the right on a tablet, or dragging the mouse to the bottom right of the screen on a PC – and type the film's name. As you type, matching movies will appear in the results below.

To buy a movie from Microsoft, you'll need a Microsoft account (see opposite). Movies can be expensive, with the latest releases costing as much as £15 or more for HD versions. Standard-definition films are cheaper, but unless you plan to watch the movie over and over, consider renting it (see Step 3). Films often arrive as a download and a stream, which means you don't need to wait for the whole file to download before you can start watching – a blessing on slower internet connections.

③ RENT A MOVIE Many films can be rented as well as bought. Indeed, for some titles it's the only option. Rental movies come in both SD and HD varieties, and are offered either as a download (where the entire film is downloaded to your device for watching offline) or streamed over the internet. Rentals last for 14 days, or for 24 hours after you first hit the play button on the movie, whichever comes sooner. They're generally much cheaper than buying the film outright, with older movies often available for only £2 or £3.

④ PLAY BACK ON XBOX If you have one of Microsoft's games consoles on your home network, you may notice the option to Play on Xbox when playing back videos. This allows you to play movies stored on your tablet or PC through your Xbox console, so you can enjoy the film on the big screen. First, go to your Xbox's Settings menu and check that Xbox Companion is set to Available in Console Settings. You also need to go into the Settings menu on your Windows 8 device, select Homegroup and make sure the setting that allows you to share content with devices such as TVs and consoles is set to On. When this is done, you should see the Play on Xbox option when playing back movies, either by flicking your finger up from the bottom of the screen or right-clicking on the Video app. This wasn't fully operational at the time of writing, but an update to the Xbox software was expected to enable the feature.

HOW LONG?
It takes no time at all to set up Music and Video on your PC; they're already installed in Windows 8. The longest part is watching movies.

HOW HARD?
The only faintly tricky parts are setting up your Microsoft account (if you haven't already done so) and connecting your PC to your Xbox console.

3

Modern apps

Photos and Camera

Most of us have hard disks brimming with digital photos of special occasions, family holidays and nights on the town. Many people will also have photos scattered across various social networks. Windows 8 brings all these together in one very neatly presented Photos app, which you'll find pre-installed on the Start menu.

PHOTOS When you first fire up the Photos app, you'll see tiles for the various locations and online services from which the app can display and organise your images. The first tile is your Pictures Library, the photos already stored on your PC or tablet. Next is SkyDrive: if you've signed into Windows with a Microsoft account, any photos stored on your SkyDrive will be displayed here.

Next in line is Facebook. Click on the Facebook tile and – if you've not already done so – you can link your Facebook account to your PC, allowing the Photos app to display any pictures stored on the social network. Further along you'll find a similar option for the photo-sharing site, Flickr. Finally, you can also view photos stored on other PCs on your home network. Note, however, that you won't be able to access the photos saved on other PCs when you take your tablet or laptop out and about.

Tap on any of the locations and you'll see a scrollable list of folders containing your photos. Folders aren't always the best way to organise photos – what about scanning your library in chronological order, for example? That's simple. Swipe up from the bottom of the screen or right-click the mouse and select Browse by date.

You can start a slideshow from within any of the photo folders stored on your device by flicking up from the bottom of the screen or right-clicking the mouse and selecting the Slide Show icon.

It's also possible to select and share pictures with friends from within the Photos app. Simply browse to a folder and select the images you want to share by pressing or clicking on the photo and then dragging upwards until you see a little tick appear alongside it. You can select photos from different folders if you wish; Windows 8 will remember them all. When you've completed your selection of photos, open the Share charm (flick in from the right on tablets, or hover the mouse in the bottom right corner) and select which app you want to share with. You could share the photos by email, upload them to your SkyDrive or post links to them with a Twitter app you've installed from the Windows Store (see p54), for example.

Tip

You can turn your Windows 8 tablet into a digital photo frame. On the homescreen of the Photo app, you'll see a little Play button icon on the left of the screen, next to your Pictures Library. Press Play and an attractive, tiled slideshow will get underway, displaying your photos year by year, or from a particular month across all the years. It's a nice thing to leave running on the mantelpiece when friends and family are over.

HOW TO...
IMPORT AND TAKE PHOTOS

 IMPORT PHOTOS FROM A CAMERA Uploading photos taken on a digital camera to your Windows 8 PC couldn't be easier. Connect your camera via USB cable, or simply pop its memory card into the slot on your PC/tablet if you have one, and you should see a little alert box appear in the top right-hand corner of your screen. Click on this box, and you'll see the option to import your pictures to the Photo app. Select that, and you should be presented with a screen showing thumbnail images of the pictures stored on your card.

By default, Windows 8 will select all the images on the card; if you wish to make your own selection of images to import, click Clear selection and pick the images you want by pressing or clicking on the photo and dragging upwards. When you're happy with your selection, click Import and the photos will be transferred to your PC.

TAKING YOUR OWN PHOTOS If you have a Windows 8 tablet, or a conventional PC or laptop with a webcam, you can take photos using the Camera app. Go to the Windows Start menu and click on Camera and the screen will be filled with a live view of what's currently in front of your camera's lens – most probably you! If you're using a tablet with both a front and rear camera, you can swipe up from the bottom of the screen and select the Change Camera option to use the rear-mounted camera. When you've lined up your subject, press anywhere on the screen to take the photo.

The image will be saved to the Camera Roll folder, which you can access via the Photos app.

 TWEAKING OPTIONS Flick up from the bottom of the screen while you're taking a photo and you'll see various camera settings you can fiddle with. Click the Spanner icon to tweak the camera's resolution settings. Use the highest possible resolution for the best-quality images, although be aware that these will take up more storage space on your device. Lower the resolution if you only want to send a quick photo via email. At the foot of the screen, you'll also notice a Timer option. Select this, and when you press the screen to take a photo you'll be given a three-second countdown to get yourself into position when taking self-portraits.

TAKE A VIDEO The Camera app can also be used to record short videos, such as a message for the family while you're away from home. Select Video Mode, and go to Camera Settings to tweak the video quality. Tablet cameras may allow you to shoot in 1080p Full HD, but that may be overkill for a basic video message, and the file size will quickly grow to tens, if not hundreds, of megabytes, so it will take longer to send the video by email or upload it to YouTube. Start and stop recording by tapping on the screen. Confusingly, videos are saved to the Camera Roll folder in Photos, not in the Videos folder.

HOW LONG?
Getting started with Photos and Camera takes no time at all – they're already installed on your Windows 8 machine.

HOW HARD?
There's nothing challenging here. Microsoft makes it simple to browse, import and share photos or videos.

News, Sport, Finance and Travel

Most of the apps that are pre-installed by default with Windows 8 are utilities – that is, apps such as Mail, Photos and SkyDrive which perform specific tasks and functions. The News, Sport, Finance and Travel apps are different beasts altogether. They're information dashboards, delivering reports and live data directly to your device's screen.

Although at first glance they may seem fairly simple, self-explanatory apps, they all include some well-concealed features that make them altogether more powerful than you might at first think.

NEWS Like all the apps here, News opens with a large, almost full-screen photo accompanying the lead item of the day. Scroll to the right, and you'll find listings of further stories broken down into categories such as World, UK, Entertainment, Sci-Tech and so on. Click on a headline and picture, and you get to read the full story, with text flowed into columns to make it more readable on devices such as widescreen tablets and laptops.

So far, so straightforward. However, flick your finger up from the bottom of the News screen or right-click with your mouse button, and some of that hidden power starts to reveal itself. The My News section, for example, lets you create bespoke news channels based on a particular topic – such as Syria, or the Labour Party. To create a news channel, click My News | Add A Section, and type the name of the subject you want to read stories on. As soon as you click Enter, the News app will scour its sources for news on

that topic and present the most recent stories in the My News section. You can create multiple news channels.

You can also choose to read the news only from particular sources. So, whether you're a fan of *The Guardian* or *The Financial Times*, click on the Sources button and you'll receive a tailored news feed exclusively from that newspaper.

SPORT The Sport app is designed in a very similar fashion to News, and has a number of excellent features for sports fans. Flick up with your finger or right-click the mouse and you can, for example, pick a favourite football team to follow, although in the UK this is rather crudely limited to Premier League football teams. Once you've selected your team, data will appear when you scroll to the right on the Sport home page. Click on the club's tile and you'll get a swathe of data about your team, including the latest results and fixtures, top scorers and a player roster.

Sport covers more than just football. Flick down from the top of the screen or right mouse click and you can take your pick from a variety of sports. The Formula One section, for example, has the full results from the latest race, the latest championship standings and motor racing news. Golf fans, meanwhile, are treated to live leaderboards from ongoing tournaments around the world, schedules and the latest player stats.

Click the All Sports button and you can choose which sports you see in the app, so if you don't care about NFL but want to keep an eye on the Italian football, for example, you can do so from here.

Tip

 If you're interested in foreign news or sport, you can change the default location for these apps. Open the relevant app, then access its Settings charm with a flick in from the right on tablets, or by hovering the mouse in the bottom-right corner, and pick Options. From there you can change the default location and language of the app.

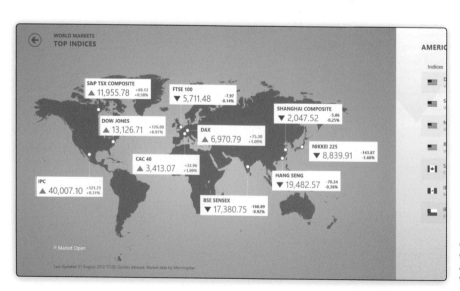

Get the latest data from stock markets around the world with the Finance app.

Above and top right:
The Sport app keeps you
abreast of all the latest
sports news, and you
can customise it to show
news from your favourite
football team.

Right: Check out the Travel
app and you'll never be
lost in France (or anywhere
else, for that matter) again.

HOW LONG?

The apps are pre-installed
so there's no work to
do. You might lose a
few hours browsing them,
however!

HOW HARD?

There's nothing
technically challenging in
these easy-to-use apps.

FINANCE Finance is the most powerful of the three dashboard apps. It delivers financial news in a similar fashion to News and Sport, but it also covers a lot more besides. Scroll to the right from the Finance home screen and you're immediately met with an interactive graph, showing how the various markets are performing. You can switch between the FTSE 100, FTSE 250 and FTSE ALL markets, and you can see how the market has performed over the past day, week, month or year.

Keep scrolling, and after the news you'll find a Watchlist of shares. Here you can enter the stocks you want to keep an eye on from the markets around the world, helping you to keep abreast of the latest movements in your portfolio. Click on that company's tile, and you'll again be presented with an interactive graph showing the company's share price performance over varying periods of time, plus the latest financial news about the firm and a barrage of other financial performance metrics.

If you're planning a trip abroad, the Currencies section of the Finance app – accessed by dragging your finger from the bottom of the screen or right-clicking with the mouse – could be very useful. This provides a matrix showing how the pound is performing against key currencies, such as the dollar and the euro. It also provides a converter that allows you to enter an amount in the home or foreign currency and convert it – handy if you're buying from an American website, for example.

TRAVEL If you're planning a trip abroad, you may want to consult the Travel app first. This contains guides to dozens of popular destinations all over the world, and it includes local information, maps, the latest exchange rate for that particular country, photos and – most impressive of all – interactive 360-degree panoramas of key tourist spots in each destination. The panoramas really come to life on a tablet, where you can smoothly scroll around the destination with a flick of the finger.

The Travel app has more practical features, too. The flight finder, for example, allows you to search for the cheapest deals to your destination. You don't even need to tell Windows where you want to fly from – simply tap the crosshairs icon in the From field and it will use location data to hunt down your nearest airport. The flight finder not only gives you a choice of airlines, but shows the latest prices from a variety of sites, so you can get the best deal.

Similarly, the app offers a hotel-booking service and, once again, you can explore 360-degree panoramas of several leading hotels to get a feel for the place before you part with your cash.

If you're visiting a particular destination, you can pin its guide to the Start menu so that when you take your tablet or laptop on your travels you'll be able to find the guide easily. Just browse to that particular destination, flick your finger from the bottom of the screen or right-click the mouse and choose Pin to Start.

3

Modern apps

WINDOWS 8 INCLUDES TWO APPS TO HELP YOU FIND THINGS, WHETHER IT'S A
DESTINATION ON A MAP OR USEFUL INFORMATION ON THE WEB

Bing Maps and Search

Microsoft's Bing brand offers many of the services more usually associated with Google, including a very respectable search engine and an online mapping facility. Here we'll reveal how to make the most of the Maps application, while on the page opposite our step-by-step walkthrough reveals the clever features inside the Bing Search app. You'll find both of these apps pre-installed on the Windows 8 Start menu.

BING MAPS One of the best things about mobile devices is that you don't have to print out maps or directions for wherever you're going: you can simply look it up on your tablet or laptop when you get close to your destination. Bear in mind, however, that you'll need an active internet connection to get fresh directions or map locations from Bing Maps, whether that's from a 3G SIM card embedded in your laptop or tablet, a local Wi-Fi hotspot or from tethering your Windows 8 device to your smartphone.

If you find yourself lost or in need of directions, Bing Maps can help out in an instant. Simply open the app, flick up from the bottom of the screen on a tablet or right-click the mouse and click on the My Location button. Bing Maps should be able to locate you within a few metres

of your precise position. Tablets and laptops fitted with a GPS chip will provide greater accuracy, but in built-up towns and cities you should be precisely located from local Wi-Fi hotspots or 3G masts.

If you need to find your way to an address, hit the Directions button. By default, Bing will use your current location as the starting point for your route. Punch an address, or preferably a postcode, into the To field, and Bing will give you turn-by-turn directions to your destination.

The directions are displayed in a strip across the top of the screen. Scroll left to move to the next step, and click on each individual direction to see it highlighted on the map. It's no replacement for a dedicated GPS app, but it's handy in an emergency.

If you're driving to your destination, Bing Maps can also help you avoid delays with the help of its Show Traffic function. Roads marked in yellow or orange are currently experiencing traffic jams, while those marked in red are heavily congested.

Finally, if you want to get a feel for a place before you arrive – a holiday destination, say – you can switch the map to Aerial View using the Map Style button and view overhead satellite photography of the area.

Tip

If Bing Maps can't locate your position, it may be because your privacy settings are preventing the app from using the necessary location data. To rectify this, head to the main PC Settings menu by going to the Start screen, opening the Settings charm and clicking Change PC settings at the bottom of the pane that appears. Then head to Privacy and check that "Let apps use my location" is set to On.

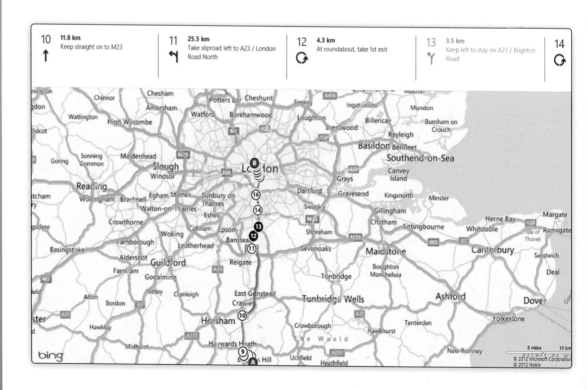

HOW TO...
MASTER BING SEARCH

① WEB AND IMAGE SEARCH The Bing Search app bears the same attractive appearance as the Bing.com search engine. When you first open it, you're presented with a full-screen, annotated image of the day, with little facts hidden behind the transparent boxes overlaid on the image. Click or prod the little boxes to uncover the facts, and swipe right to see previous images.

To perform a search, simply type the query into the blank box and the results will be returned in tiles; click the relevant tile to open an Internet Explorer page. Results are broken down into Websites and Images. Click the latter and thumbnail image results appear. Click on an individual image and it opens a full-screen slideshow, allowing you to swipe or scroll effortlessly to the next image search result.

② DOCK BING RESULTS IN A SIDE PANEL One of Bing's cleverest features is that it lets you keep your search results in a panel down the side of the screen while you view the website the results refer to in the main part of the screen. This allows you to jump from one result to the next until you find the information you desire. To dock the results on the side of the screen, first type your search query as described above. If you're using a mouse, click and hold at the top of the screen until a hand appears, then drag the search results to either side of the screen until it snaps to a panel. You can then click on the results to open an Internet Explorer window in the remaining part of the screen. On a tablet it's a little trickier:

here you have to drag your finger in slowly from the left-hand side of the screen until the screen is divided in two by a bar. You can then drag the dividing bar until your Bing results appear in a thin strip down either side.

③ SHARING IMAGE RESULTS Having performed a search, you might want to share an image via email or on Twitter or Facebook. To do this in Windows 8: click on the image result so that it's displayed full screen, then open the Share charm by swiping a finger from the right of the screen on a tablet, or hovering the mouse in the bottom right-hand corner. Click Share and you'll be presented with a list of apps you can use to share the image. Pick Mail, for example, and the image result will be automatically embedded in a message for you; just enter the recipient's address and any accompanying subject line or message. You can do likewise with normal web search results opened in Internet Explorer.

④ TURNING ON SAFE SEARCH If you want to have search results filtered so that they don't contain adult images or foul language, you can do so. Open the Bing Search app and open the Settings charm, in the same manner as described in Step 3. Select SafeSearch and you'll have three levels of protection to choose from. It's set to Moderate filtering by default, but you may wish to beef it up or switch it off altogether. Be warned: no search filter is ever 100% effective.

HOW LONG?
Both apps are pre-installed, and it takes no time at all to master the features of either.

HOW HARD?
There's nothing technically challenging here, although creating split-screen search results is fiddly on a tablet.

 THE WINDOWS STORE CONTAINS THOUSANDS OF FREE AND PAID-FOR APPS THAT WILL ENHANCE YOUR WINDOWS 8 EXPERIENCE

Introducing the Windows Store

All the apps we've profiled so far in this chapter have been made by Microsoft and come pre-installed with the Windows 8 operating system. However, there are thousands of other apps available from third-party developers that will make your computer or tablet a much more interesting and capable device. Many of these apps are free, while others you'll have to pay for. They're all available from the Windows Store, which is Microsoft's answer to Apple's App Store and the Google Play store.

BROWSING THE STORE You'll find a button for the Windows Store on the Start screen. Once you're in, you'll notice it has a similar layout to the Start screen itself. Apps are broken into different categories – ranging from fun sections such as Games, to the rather more dry-sounding Government section – that you can browse by scrolling right along the Store.

A good place to Start is the Top Free tile, which you should see as soon as you open the Store. This allows you to experiment with browsing and installing applications, without it costing you a penny.

The Windows Store contains two different types of apps: Modern (or what used to be called Metro) Apps,

and the traditional desktop apps that will probably be familiar from previous versions of Windows. You can tell them apart by their listings. Modern apps will either be listed as "free" or with a price tag. Desktop apps have the label "Desktop app" instead of a price.

The reason for this is that you can't buy desktop apps directly from the Windows Store. Microsoft is merely listing these apps, and foists you off to the publisher's website if you want to buy the software. It's hardly the ideal shopping experience, but it's Microsoft's imperfect way of keeping traditional Windows software publishers onside, while it emphasises the new-fangled Modern apps in its Windows 8 Store.

Any Modern app you buy from Microsoft can be installed on up to five other PCs or tablets, as long as you use the same Microsoft account login on both machines. The downside is that apps paid for and installed using one user account are not installed in other accounts on the same PC, meaning you'll have to pay twice if you want two users to have access to a game, for example. This is pure stupidity on Microsoft's part, because it encourages families to all use the PC using the same account, with all the inherent insecurity that brings.

Tip

◢ When deciding which apps to install from the Windows Store, look for the five-star rating under each app's name. This is the average score awarded to the app by people who've previously installed and used it.

HOW TO...
BUY AND INSTALL MODERN APPS

CHOOSE YOUR APP Click on the Store icon on Start menu and browse the Store for apps. If you want to search for a particular app by name, open the Search charm (swipe from the right of the screen on a tablet or hover the mouse in the bottom right-hand corner) and type the name of the app you're looking for.

In each app's listing you can scroll through screengrabs of the app and read through other people's reviews before making your decision. Also check the Details tab – this tells you what specification your PC will need to run the app. The vast majority of Modern apps should run on any Windows 8 device.

BUY OR TRY If the app is free, you can simply click the Install button and the app will begin to download and install on your device. If it isn't, you'll see a Buy button below the price, or maybe even a Try button, which allows you to download a fully functioning version of the app that will expire after a set period of time, normally a day or two. This allows you to get a feel for the app before parting with your cash.

If you haven't already linked your Microsoft account with your credit card details (Xbox Live users should find this done for them), then you'll need to enter your payment details. You should be prompted to do this the first time you try to buy an app, but if not, open the Settings charm (flick from the right on a tablet, or hover the mouse in the bottom right), select Your Account and enter your payment details. When an app has finished installing, its tile will appear on the Windows Start screen.

INSTALL APPS BOUGHT ON OTHER MACHINES Microsoft allows you to install Modern apps on up to five machines, providing you sign in with the same Microsoft account on all the devices. Apps aren't automatically synchronised from machine to machine, however, so you'll have to install them manually.

To find apps you've already paid for on another machine, enter the Store, swipe down from the top of the screen or right-click, and select Your Apps. Here you'll find a comprehensive list of all the apps – paid for and free – that you've acquired previously on your account. Simply click on the app's tile to select it for installation – you can select as many as you like in one go – and click Install.

INSTALL UPDATES Developers will periodically update the apps installed on your machine.

You'll know that updates are available when you see a small number appear in the Windows Store's live tile, denoting how many updates are available. To upgrade to the latest version of these apps, enter the Store, click on the Updates link in the top right-hand corner of the page and choose to either install some or all of the updates. You won't be charged to upgrade to the latest version of paid-for apps. Return to the Start screen and click on the app's tile to check out any new features.

HOW LONG?
The length of time it takes to download and install apps depends on their size and the speed of your internet connection.

HOW HARD?
Once you've set up your payment account details, the rest is plain-sailing.

 WE PICK OUR HIGHLIGHTS FROM THE WINDOWS STORE TO HELP YOU CHOOSE WHICH APPS TO INSTALL WHEN YOU UPGRADE TO THE NEW OS

20 of the best Modern apps

◀ **Flight Aware** This flight tracker provides an almost terrifying visual guide to the planes in the sky over our major airports. It plots the routes taken by aircraft over nearby airports, and allows you to click on the plane for details of when it departed and any delays suffered on its route. More usefully, it allows you to enter a flight number and plot the flight's progress on the map; handy if you're collecting someone from the airport. It brings live data on airport delays, and how long you can expect to be stuck in the lounge.

▶ **MetroTwit** Metro Twit is by far the best Twitter client we've seen for Windows 8 so far. Split into neat columns showing your timeline, mentions and direct messages, Metro Twit makes it easy to keep abreast of the latest goings-on. Unlike Microsoft's People app, MetroTwit allows you to scan your timeline by scrolling vertically, rather than horizontally, which feels much more natural, and it's far less wasteful of screen space. Our only complaint is a lack of live tile updates on the Start screen, but hopefully that will come in an update.

◀ **Armed** A real-time strategy game in the ilk of the classic PC game Starcraft, Armed is proof that Modern Windows 8 apps won't lack substance. Equally manageable either on a touchscreen tablet or using a mouse on a traditional computer, Armed requires you to build a base, harvest resources, defend your settlement against attack and explore new territories. It's a little complicated to wade straight into either single or multiplayer gameplay, but the excellent tutorial shows you the ropes.

Tip

◢ Can't find your app on the Windows Start screen? Simply begin typing its name on the Start screen and it will appear in the search results. Alternatively, swipe a finger up from the bottom of the Start screen on tablets, or right-click with a mouse, and click on the All Apps button that appears to get an alphabetically ordered list of every app on your PC.

▶ **Ministry of Sound** A must-have application for fans of the legendary dance club, the Ministry of Sound app provides a wealth of free music sessions for clubbers. The Live From The Club section provides a five-hour set from the previous Saturday night, giving you a feel for the atmosphere of the London venue. The app also features pre-recorded sets from well-known DJs such as Sister Bliss. If you like the free music on offer, there's also an opportunity to preview and download the club's huge back catalogue of albums via the app.

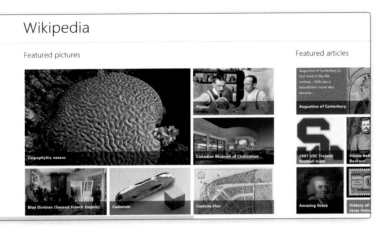

Wikipedia

Featured pictures

Featured articles

▲ Sky News The Sky News app has in-depth text and video reports on the breaking news of the day. Text flows awkwardly on larger PC monitors, but the full-screen video reports give you a three-minute bulletin of the day's major news, the latest weather forecast or a live feed of the Sky News channel, provided you have an internet connection.

▲ Wikipedia This app provides a more convenient way to browse Wikipedia, particularly on tablets. The homescreen highlights featured images and articles of the day, which provide a fun way to dip into random topics. However, to search for articles, you'll need to use the Search charm – activated by swiping a finger from the right of the screen on tablets. You'll need a live net connection to perform searches.

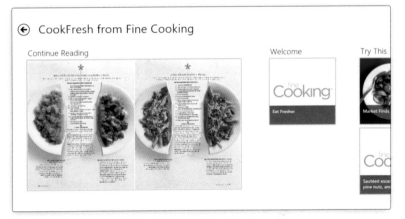

▲ Cocktail Flow A fantastic app for those with a drinks cabinet full of half-empty bottles. Click on the Cabinet section and tell the app what spirits, liqueurs and mixers you have, and it will provide you with a list of cocktails for those ingredients. You can also pick a cocktail from the catalogue and it will show you how to mix it.

▲ Fine Cooking Fine Cooking magazine provides a variety of ways to digest its content. You can browse the contents using the Windows 8 tiled interface, but when you click on an article or recipe, you can view it as a scan of the magazine page or as plain text and photos. The different viewing options are activated by swiping up from the foot of the screen on tablets, or with a right-click of the mouse.

▼ Pinball FX2 Touchscreen tablets are perfect for pinball: you merely tap on either side of the screen to operate the flippers. Pinball FX 2 isn't the most impressive

pinball app we've seen, but it has some great features, not least the ability to see how your scores compare to your friends on Xbox Live, as well as online tournaments. You get one free table, but others will have to be purchased.

▲ Kindle Kindle owners aren't restricted to reading books on their e-reader. Amazon has released Kindle apps for lots of smartphones and tablets, and now Windows 8 joins the party. Books are automatically synchronised to the last read page, and there are options to adjust font sizes and page colours for those with eyesight difficulties. Annoyingly, the Store jumps straight to the US site, though.

OneNote MX OneNote is Microsoft's much underrated note-taking application, and it's one of the first of the company's apps to get a proper touchscreen makeover. You can tap notes using the onscreen keyboard, and then use the smart radial-dial controls to add more fancy features, such as tables, images that you've taken with the tablet's camera or tags to help you find the notebook at a later date.

Fresh Paint An app to bring out your artistic side, Fresh Paint brilliantly re-creates the feel of splashing paint on canvas. Dab away with your fingers onscreen using a variety of brushes and watch as colours merge in a scarily lifelike manner, because you forgot to "dry" the canvas before adding the next layer. It's a wonderfully fun way to create electronic paintings, and not all that difficult for even bumbling amateurs to create something half-decent.

Music Maker Jam A terrific timewaster, Music Maker Jam allows you to blend together your own Dubstep, Jazz or House music, simply by playing with a range of sliders and effects. You get to choose which instruments and vocals appear on your tracks and how much emphasis to afford to each, and once you've got the balance right you can start experimenting with key changes and writing your own loops. The resulting soundtracks are awesome, especially when played back through speakers.

Flash Cards An app for the younger members of the household, Flash Cards helps your kids with their mental arithmetic, popping up maths questions from a series of disciplines, such as adding, subtraction, multiplication and so on. They then have to tap the answer using the big onscreen numbers. The quizzes are timed, and the challenge is to beat their best scores, both in accuracy and speed of answers. The default 30 questions per quiz is perhaps a little tiring, but you can adjust the number of questions in Settings.

Barcode Generator The misleadingly named Barcode Generator actually generates QR codes – the grids seen on billboards and in magazines – for personal use. It can create codes for your email address, Twitter account, YouTube video or Facebook page, providing a quick and easy way to help promote your business.

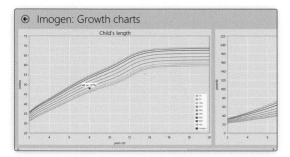

Growth Tracker A smart utility for parents of young children, Growth Tracker allows you to monitor the height and weight of your child at regular intervals and see how they compare to the averages for their age. The Height Predictor will even take a stab at how tall they're going to be in adulthood. There's a one-child trial version of the app available; a mere £1.39 if you like what you see.

Feed Reader RSS feeds have fallen out of fashion in the age of social networks, but there's still a hard core of users out there. If you're a Google Reader fan, check out Feed Reader (free trial, £2.99 thereafter), a cleanly presented viewer for your chosen feeds. It includes all the usual features, including the option to "Star" articles.

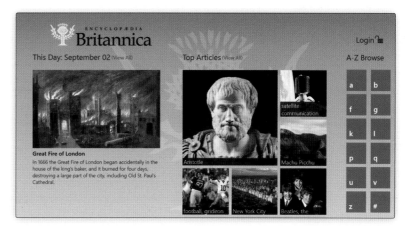

Encyclopaedia Britannica The stalwart of the encyclopaedia world has delivered a very smart Windows 8 app. It's free, although you'll need to be a Britannica subscriber to read full articles. The best feature is the Link Map, which creates an interactive tree of related articles that virtually begs you to read around the topic. The app's presentation is also a notch above that of the free Wikipedia's.

Awesome Picture A free photo editor that allows you to apply a selection of basic effects to images, such as adding a sepia tint or brightening the photo as a whole. There's also a smattering of drawing tools, allowing you to highlight parts of the image with circles or arrows. It's rudimentary, and we expect there are better photos editors to come, but it won't cost you a penny.

National Rail Enquires This app is a useful way to keep an eye on what the trains are up to before you set off for the station. It allows you to set both Home and Work stations, and then provides live departure boards from each, so you can see if the delays are mounting on your line. For advanced journey planning, though, you're dumped into the National Rail Enquiries website.

IN THIS CHAPTER

62 Introducing the desktop
Find out where all the Windows desktop features lie, and what all those little icons do, with our annotated guide.

64 Windows Explorer
The Windows Explorer has been given a new look with the ribbon interface. Find out how to tap into its many powers.

66 Personalise the desktop
Make the Windows desktop look just how you like it using your own wallpapers, themes and colours. We'll show you how it's done.

68 Advanced desktop shortcuts
If you really want to master Windows, you need to learn the various desktop shortcuts. Get to know them better with our eight-point guide.

70 Mastering Jump Lists
Jump Lists are a quick and easy way to go straight to the files, documents and application features you need. We explain all.

72 The Task Manager
Find out how to spot trouble brewing on your PC before it's too late with our guide to the revamped Windows 8 Task Manager.

4
Windows desktop

THE WINDOWS D

Windows 8 may have seen the traditional Windows desktop relegated in favour of the sparkling new Modern Start screen, but rest assured: it remains a pivotal part of the operating system – especially for those still using traditional desktop computers or laptops without a touchscreen. And Microsoft hasn't neglected the desktop in this latest refresh, either:

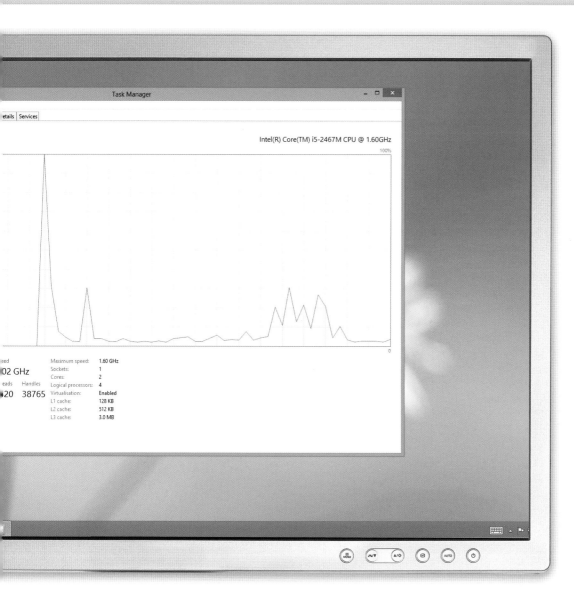

ESKTOP

Windows Explorer has a fresh new look, and a complete overhaul of the Task Manager has delivered an across-the-board improvement to this all-important suite of utilities. There are a few new additions worth a mention too, while popular recent Windows additions such as Jump Lists have been retained. We explain how to use them all.

THE WINDOWS DESKTOP OF OLD IS STILL THERE IN WINDOWS 8, BUT HAS CHANGED SIGNIFICANTLY. OUR ANNOTATED GUIDE DETAILS THE CHANGES

Introducing the Windows desktop

1 **Pinned applications** give you a fast-track to your favourite programs in Windows 8, enabling you to launch your favourite applications with a single click. Simply right-click on a program's icon and select "Pin this program to Taskbar". Right-clicking also displays the Jump List – a list of recently accessed files and other useful commands.

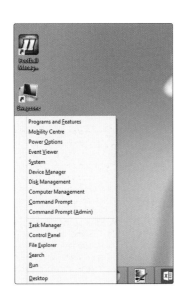

Tip

If you really can't live without a Start button on your Windows desktop, you can download unofficial patches that bring it back. Our favourite is Classic Shell (http://classicshell.sourceforge.net), which returns the Start button to its familiar spot on the bottom left of the Taskbar.

2 The **Administrator tasks menu** is effectively a replacement for the Start button and can be accessed by pressing the Windows key and X simultaneously on your keyboard. This pops up the Administrator Tasks menu, which provides one-click access to a number of handy features, including the Control Panel, Task Manager and Programs and Features, from where you can uninstall traditional desktop software.

3 The **Recycle Bin** is where files are sent before they are permanently expunged from your PC. Every time you delete a file, it's first sent to this holding area in case it was deleted by mistake. For that reason, it's important to empt the Recycle Bin regularly to avoid unwanted files hogging disk space unnecessarily. If you find you have deleted a file in Windows Explorer accidentally, click on the file in the Recycle Bin and click "Restore the selected items" to return it safely back to its original location.

7 To **personalise the desktop**, right-click on any unoccupied space on the desktop and select "Personalise the desktop". This allows you to adjust the background image that appears on your screen, or select a theme which scrolls through multiple different desktop backgrounds throughout the day. A new feature in Windows 8 is the option to stretch a desktop image across two monitors should you have a dual-display setup.

6 **Charms** may be predominantly associated with the new-look Modern UI start screen, but they're also accessible directly from the old Windows desktop. They're opened in the same way, too: either by sliding a finger from the right edge of the screen on a touchscreen device, or by hovering the mouse in the bottom-right corner of the screen. Click Settings for the option to switch off or restart your PC.

4 The **clock and date** are largely self-explanatory, but you may not know that you can left-click on the time and get the option of a secondary clock to display – which is handy if you work in different locations internationally. Click the clock, then "Change time and date settings", then click on the Additional Clocks tab, select the appropriate time zone and give the clock a name (New York, for example). Click Apply to finish, and then whenever you left-click on the clock, your secondary clock will appear alongside the current time and calendar.

5 The **Notifications Area** is where Windows alerts you to activities or problems with your PC. The little white flag is the Action Center, where you will periodically be prompted to install updates or back up your system. The power plug/battery symbol reveals remaining battery life on laptops/tablets, and can be used to adjust power settings. Other symbols include Wi-Fi network signal strength and volume controls. To tailor what appears in the Notifications Area, click on the little up arrow.

Windows Explorer

Windows Explorer – the menu system you use to access the files and folders on your PC – has remained largely unchanged across several versions of Microsoft's operating system up to Windows 7. That's no longer the case now that Windows 8 is here, with some significant changes having given this fundamental operating system tool a whole new look and feel.

THE RIBBON The biggest change is the introduction of the ribbon interface, which you may already be familiar with from recent versions of Microsoft Office. For the uninitiated, the ribbon puts common tasks and features in tabs at the top of the window, making it easier to find features that were previously buried in drop-down menus. The ribbon has its fans and critics, but in the case of Windows 8, it certainly makes it simpler to perform common tasks such as selecting a group of files and moving them to a new folder, without having to juggle multiple windows or learn keyboard shortcuts.

The ribbon is a context-sensitive menu system. In plain English that means features only become available when they're relevant or needed. For example, when you first click on the Windows Explorer icon in the Taskbar, you'll notice that buttons such as Copy and Paste are greyed out. The reason is obvious enough: you haven't selected anything that can be copied or pasted yet! Similarly, only when you click on a photo does a new tab called Picture Tools appear, containing commonly used editing tools that allow you to rotate the photo and perform other tasks that are only applicable to images.

It's a change of approach that will affect how you use Windows Explorer from the ground up, but it's by no means the only one. There are other, admittedly more minor, changes that are also worth a mention. Microsoft has finally listened to common sense and reintroduced the Up level button (the little up arrow next to the bar containing the file path of the folder you're currently looking at), making it easier to return to a parent folder.

The Search facility has also been enhanced by the ribbon interface. If you type a search term in the Windows Explorer search box it will, by default, search the contents of the library or folder you've currently got open. However, as soon as you click in the search box, you'll notice that a Search Tools tab appears, allowing you to refine the search further, such as only including files that have been modified in the past week, or only files of a certain size or type. This makes finding files that were accidentally saved in the wrong location much easier.

Windows Explorer will automatically choose the view option best suited to the type of file you're browsing, such as thumbnails for images.

HOW TO...
CUSTOMISE WINDOWS EXPLORER

① CHANGE FILE LISTINGS Windows Explorer is quite intelligent in the way that it displays files. Photographs, by default, are displayed as thumbnails, while documents – where there's normally little to be gained in seeing a thumbnail – are listed by filename. However, you can change how you view the contents of a folder if this doesn't suit – you might, for instance, want to browse larger thumbnails when searching for a particular photo in a folder. To do this, open the folder in question and then click on the View tab and choose "Extra Large Icons". Large icons can also come in handy for items other than photographs. When you're browsing Explorer with your fingertips on a tablet, for instance, tapping individual file listings can be quite tricky. Switch your documents to be displayed as extra large icons and it's much easier to drag and drop them into a new folder.

② SORT AND GROUP FILES By default, Windows 8 sorts folders in alphabetical order, based on their filename. If you're viewing a folder containing dozens or hundreds of files, for instance, that might not be the best way to find the specific file you're looking for. Click on the View tab and click the "Sort by" button, and a number of different options will come into play. You can sort by date modified to send documents you have worked on recently to the top of the list, or sort by size to identify big files that are taking up huge chunks of disk space – which is a particularly useful option on tablets with a limited quantity of storage space. Alongside "Sort

by", you'll also see a "Group by" button that allows you to collate your files using the same criteria. So, for example, if you choose to group by Name, the files will be segregated into groups of filenames starting with A-H, I-P and so on, to make them easier to browse.

③ CHECK BOXES One new feature you may have noticed in Windows 8 Explorer is the addition of little checkboxes alongside every folder and file. These are turned on by default on tablet/touchscreen devices and are intended to make it easier to make a selection of non-consecutive files to copy, paste or move to another folder. Frankly, we're not sure the little checkboxes make that process any easier, and they tend to get in the way when you're using a mouse and keyboard to navigate Explorer and not a touchscreen. Fortunately, they are easily switched off. In Explorer, simply click the View tab and untick the "Item Check Boxes" entry.

④ HIDE THE RIBBON As we mentioned opposite, not everyone is a fan of the ribbon interface. It's not possible to switch the ribbon off, but you can choose for it to be hidden from view if you're an advanced users who's comfortable using keyboard shortcuts. In an Explorer window, click on the down arrow icon in the top left of the window, and select "Minimise the ribbon" from the drop-down menu that appears. Alternatively, click on the little up arrow on the far right of the screen, next to the question mark in a blue circle.

HOW LONG?
It won't take long to master the new Explorer despite the variety of new options on offer.

HOW HARD?
For all but the most hardcore of PC users who are steeped in keyboard shortcuts, this new look should make life easier.

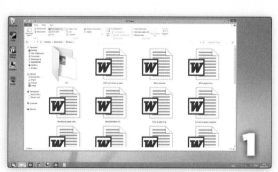

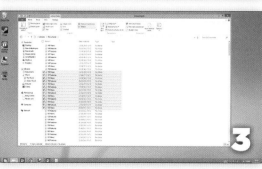

4
Windows desktop

Personalise the Windows desktop

Most people like to stamp their personality on their PC by adjusting the appearance of the desktop. The good news is Windows 8 makes it easy to add a splash of character.

Many of its customisation features can be found by right-clicking on the desktop and selecting Personalise. You can also access these settings via the Control Panel, which you can open by holding down the Windows Key and pressing X, then selecting the relevant option. The simplest way to start tinkering is to use Windows 8's themes, as we explain on the opposite page. But there are a few basics you should be aware of before getting stuck in.

THE TASKBAR The bar at the bottom of the screen is largely identical to that of Windows 7, with big chunky icons for the programs currently open on your PC. If you want to go back to the old Windows XP/Vista layout of text labels and icons, right-click on the Taskbar, click Properties, and select "Never combine" from the Taskbar buttons drop-down menu.

The best thing about the Taskbar is that even programs that aren't currently in use can be shown here, giving you one-click access to your favourite software. To add a program to the Taskbar, open the program, then right-click on its icon and choose "Pin this program to Taskbar".

You can also tweak how the icons on the Taskbar are ordered, grouping similar applications together, for instance. To do this, left-click and hold on a Taskbar icon and drag into your desired position before releasing. The icon will now stay there for good. The Taskbar itself can be relocated too: move it to the top or either side of the screen by right-clicking on the Taskbar, choosing Properties and taking your pick from the Taskbar location drop-down menu.

DESKTOP ICONS The first time you open Windows 8, the Recycle Bin will be one of very few icons on the desktop (invariably along with a few other software icons installed by your PC manufacturer). If you want to add shortcuts to your favourite software here, go to the new Start menu, right-click on the application's tile, click "Open file location" from the menu that appears at the bottom, then right-click on the program's name and click "Create shortcut".

DISPLAY RESOLUTION Windows 8 should select the correct screen resolution automatically, but if it looks fuzzy or you want to experiment, right-click an empty space on the desktop, select Screen Resolution then make your desired change using the sliding scale. If you pick an unusable option, Windows gives you 15 seconds to revert back to your previous display settings before applying the change.

Tip

Today's widescreen monitors offer very high resolutions, which can make onscreen text so fine as to be almost unreadable. There's no need to artificially bump down the screen resolution – Windows 8 allows you to make text bigger instead.
1 Right-click on the desktop, choose Screen Resolution and then click on the link "Make text and other items larger or smaller".
2 Choose from the options to make the text and other items either 125% or 150% of their current size. You will need to restart your PC for the changes to take effect.
3. Now Windows text and desktop icons will look larger, without any loss of clarity or sharpness to the screen as a whole.

The Windows 8 Taskbar gives instant access to your favourite programs and files – you can even personalise their order on screen.

HOW TO...
CHOOSE OR CREATE A THEME

1 **CHOOSE A THEME** Windows 8 comes with a series of default themes – ready-made packages of complementary desktop backgrounds, sounds and screensavers. These include a theme based around the Earth and one on flowers. Pick by right-clicking on the desktop, choosing Personalise and selecting one of the Aero Themes. Each theme contains a selection of photos, and your background will change periodically as it cycles through them. To move on to the next photo, right-click on the desktop and choose "Next desktop background".

2 **DOWNLOAD NEW THEMES** Microsoft has also put together a series of alternative themes, available to download. In the Personalise menu, click "Get more themes online" at the far right. Early examples include a beautiful set of Forest scenes. Click on themes to download them to your computer. Once downloaded, they'll be available from the My Themes section.

3 **BUILD YOUR OWN THEME** Beautiful as Microsoft's Windows 8 themes are, the best way to stamp your personality on your PC is by creating your own. First, save all the photos you want in your new theme into a single Pictures folder. Now open that folder, right-click on one of the photos and choose "Set as desktop background". Close the folder, right-click on the desktop and choose Personalise: you should see your photo associated with an unsaved theme. To add the rest of your desired photos to the theme, click the Desktop Background link at the foot of the screen and browse to the folder containing the images. Select those you want to add, holding down the Ctrl button as you click them, adjust the timing settings if you like, then click Save Changes. You can also tweak the colour of the border on the desktop windows to match your photos, as well as the Windows sounds and the screensaver. When you've finished, click Save Theme and give it a name.

4 **SHARE YOUR CREATIONS** You can share your saved theme with friends and family, or upload it to a website for others to download, though you'll need to make sure you own the copyright to the photos before doing so. In the Themes menu, right-click your chosen theme and select "Save theme for sharing". Give it a name and save it. You can now email the file to other users or make it available for download. Beware: if you've used a lot of high-resolution photos, the file may be too large for some people to receive in their mailboxes.

HOW LONG?
About 15 minutes, a bit longer if you're planning to create your own theme and share it.

HOW HARD?
It's blissfully simple to tweak the appearance of your PC and share the results with others.

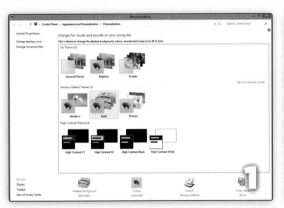

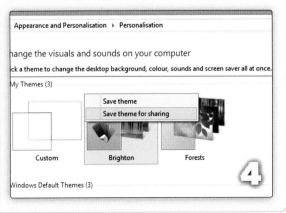

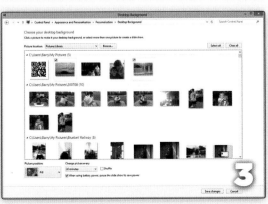

Advanced desktop shortcuts

The traditional Windows desktop has more power than you might expect. It provides a range of features that make the operating system quicker and easier to use. Many of these aren't visible at first glance – they're hidden away, only becoming apparent when you drag windows in a certain direction or activate a keyboard shortcut. On these pages, we'll show you eight secret shortcuts you can use to get even more out of Windows 8.

1
WINDOWS SHAKE Often you can find yourself with a dozen application windows open. This makes moving between programs laborious, and can distract you from the document you're working on. In Windows 8 you can easily "shake away" the clutter, minimising all the open windows except the active one.

To use this handy feature, simply click and hold on the bar at the top of the window you're working on (drag it down slightly if the window is full-screen), then shake the mouse gently from left to right.

You should see all the other windows magically disappear, leaving only the currently active window. Don't worry if you have unsaved work in any of those windows – they haven't been closed altogether, just minimised to the Taskbar at the bottom of the screen. Click on the program's icon there to re-open the window.

2
GO FULL-SCREEN If you're working in a window and want to make it full-screen, there's no need to find and click the fiddly little box icon at the top right. Just drag the window's top bar to the very top of the screen; the window instantly fills the screen. To return it to its original size, drag it back down.

3
SNAP TO THE EDGES Sometimes you only want a single window visible on the screen, but there are other times when you want to be able to work in more than one simultaneously: for example, you might need to refer to a web page while writing a document.

Windows 8 makes it easy to display two windows side by side. Click on the bar at the top of the first window you want and drag it to the far left of the screen; the window snaps into place, filling half the screen. Now do the same with the second window, but drag it to the right. The windows should be butted up.

The only time this won't work is when you have more than one monitor on your PC. In this instance, use keyboard shortcuts instead: hold down the Windows key and press the left or right arrow key as appropriate.

4
SHOW THE DESKTOP You don't have to minimise all your windows to take a peek at your desktop; just hover the mouse in the bottom-right corner and all your open windows temporarily melt away, revealing your Windows desktop and all the desktop icons that lurk beneath. Handy if you want to check a file has been saved to the desktop.

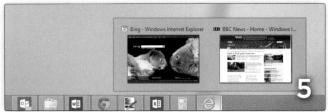

Windows 8 is a multitasker's dream, offering a range of tools to help you switch effortlessly between apps, view multiple documents side by side, and instantly access the programs and folders in the Taskbar.

5 **WINDOWS PEEK** By default, Windows 8 doesn't show names for the icons in the Taskbar, so it can sometimes be tricky to find the window you're looking for. A feature called Windows Peek can help. Hover over any icon in the Taskbar and up pops a miniature thumbnail image of its contents. Move your mouse over this thumbnail and Windows shows you the position and contents of the window itself. This is handy when you have multiple web pages open in web browsers: each tab gets its own thumbnail; just click the one you want to open.

6 **TASK SWITCHER** If you don't want to scroll through thumbnails with Peek, there's an easier way to flip through open apps. Hold down Alt and press Tab to invoke the Task Switcher. You'll now see thumbnails of all your open windows slap-bang in the middle of the screen. With Alt still held down, keep pressing Tab to cycle through to the window of your choice – or click on a thumbnail to switch directly to it.

7 **SCROLL THROUGH OPEN APPS** Another way to scroll through open applications is to hold down the Windows key and press Tab. This goes through the apps open on your system in sequence via thumbnails running down the left of the screen. However, this option only works with the new-style Modern UI apps; it won't enable you to switch between Outlook and Word, say. This replaces the little-used Flip 3D feature in Windows Vista and Windows 7.

8 **SELECT APPS BY NUMBER** If you have nine or ten different apps open, it can be a pain to cycle through all of them to get to the one you want. As an alternative, press the Windows key and 1 and the left-most app on your Taskbar will be opened or made active. Windows key + 2 will open the second app, and so on. This is particularly useful if you've pinned your favourite applications to the Taskbar and keep them in a set order.

YOU DON'T NEED TO CLUTTER YOUR DESKTOP WITH SHORTCUTS TO FILES AND FOLDERS. WITH JUMP LISTS YOU CAN FIND THEM IN A COUPLE OF CLICKS

Mastering Jump Lists

Right-click on a program's icon in the Taskbar at the foot of the screen, and you'll see a list sprout upwards – these are the so-called Jump Lists. They can also be accessed by clicking and holding on a program's icon and dragging the mouse upwards, or pressing your finger on the icon and swiping upwards if you're using a touchscreen.

In the vast majority of cases, the Jump List will feature items you've recently opened using that particular program. In Microsoft Word, for example, it's a quick way to open a document you were working on yesterday: instead of having to plough through folders to find it, just hover over the title and left-click.

With applications such as Windows Media Player, Jump Lists also give access to basic controls, such as "Resume previous list" to continue playing your music from where you last left off. Alternatively, right-click on the Internet Explorer logo and its Jump List gives you the option to start surfing in InPrivate mode, which won't leave any trace of your web session lingering on your PC. There are plenty more applications that make use of Jump Lists – just try right-clicking and see what you can find!

You also have some control over what appears in the Jump Lists. If you have a file or document that you open regularly – say, an expenses form or a welcome letter that you send out to new members of your club – you can "pin" it to the Jump List so that it's always to hand.

There are two ways of doing this. If the document you want to keep is already in the application's Jump List, click the little pin icon next to its name, which appears

when you hover the mouse over the filename in question. If it isn't, open the folder containing the relevant document and drag it down onto a blank space on the Taskbar.

It isn't only files and documents that can be pinned to Jump Lists. If there's a folder you want quick access to, you don't have to create a shortcut on your desktop: just drag its icon down into the Taskbar and onto the Windows Explorer icon (the yellow one that looks like a bunch of folders). You'll be offered the option to pin the folder there.

If you decide you don't want an item pinned to a Jump List any more, it's easy to remove: just hover over its name and click the little pin icon.

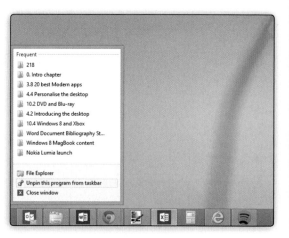

Jump Lists give one-click access to your most recently accessed files, but also allow you to perform context-sensitive tasks directly from the Taskbar. The Spotify Jump List, for example, lists the tracks you've listened to most recently, but also lets you jump straight into a playlist too.

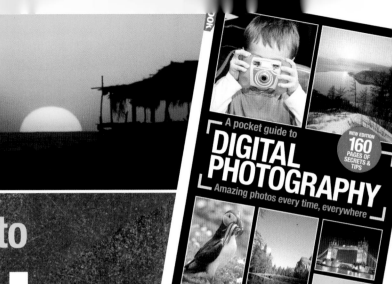

A pocket guide to
DIGITAL PHOTOGRAPHY
Amazing photos every time, everywhere

ONLY
£6.9.

ON SALE NOW!

Order your print or digital MagBook
at **magbooks.com**

4

Windows desktop

THE WINDOWS TASK MANAGER HAS BEEN OVERHAULED IN WINDOWS 8, MAKING IT MORE USEFUL FOR DIAGNOSING AND RESOLVING PROBLEMS WITH YOUR PC

The new Task Manager

On any list of cool features that you'd want to see in a new operating system, a revamped Task Manager wouldn't be a high priority for too many people. But while it's never likely to be the most glamorous of utilities, the revamped Windows 8 Task Manager will be welcomed by anyone with a keen interest on what going's on inside their PC, or who needs help identifying a problem that's reducing their system to a crawl.

BASIC VIEW When you first open the Windows Task Manager – most easily found by right-clicking in the space where the start button used to be on the desktop, or by typing "Task Manager" on the Modern UI Start screen – you'd be forgiven for thinking it has been emasculated. All that appears by default is a list of apps – both new Modern UI apps, and traditional desktop applications – currently running your PC, and the option to close them.

For tablet users, or anyone just wanting to despatch a crashed application, this may indeed be all they need. However, if you click the More Details arrow at the foot of the Task Manager, you'll find there's a lot more power lying beneath.

PROCESS MANAGER Once you've clicked on the More Details button, you'll see the Task Manager is broken into a series of tabs, the first of which is Processes. This gives you a highly detailed view of the programs and background processes that are consuming the resources on your PC. All of this

data is heatmapped, so if any program or process is being particularly greedy with your computer's CPU or memory, it will appear in a darker shade of orange than the rest.

This is particularly useful for identifying apps that are dragging down your PC. However, the list can often be quite long, so the Task Manager also allows you to sort the apps in order of how much demand they're placing on the CPU, memory, disk or network by clicking on the title of the relevant column.

Once you've identified the misbehaving app, simply click on its name and use the End Task button in the bottom right. Be aware, however, that doing so will close the application immediately, often taking any unsaved work with it. It's also worth noting that some apps, such as the Chrome web browser, will have multiple processes listed in the Task Manager, so you may need to close several entries to completely free your PC's resources.

PERFORMANCE The Performance tab is an excellent way to detect bottlenecks on your PC, and should be your first port of call if your system is stuttering or freezing. Now presented with beautifully clear graphs, the two key performance factors to keep an eye on are CPU and memory utilisation. If either of these are frequently maxing out while you're running everyday tasks, it's time to start thinking about upgrading your PC or (if possible) adding some more memory to your system. It might also suggest that a misbehaving piece of software is thrashing of all your

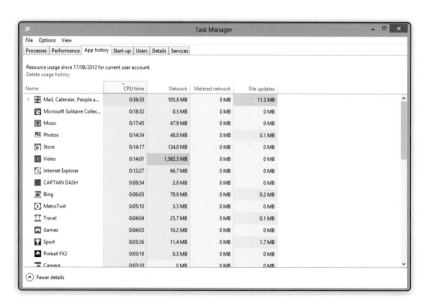

The new App History tab in the Task Manager gives you a quick overview of the impact Modern UI apps are having on your system, and how much data they are using up – an important consideration for tablet users on mobile data connections.

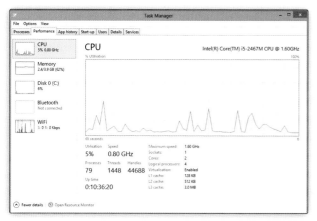

The Task Manager has been completely overhauled in Windows 8, giving you a better set of tools across the board for monitoring, analysing and tweaking your system resources and how they are used. You can adjust the level of detail from a basic list of apps (left) to more detailed heatmaps of new and old-style apps (above).

HOW LONG?
It takes no time at all to tweak Task Manager settings, but diagnostics can take a while.

HOW HARD?
The Task Manager can look a little intimidating, but it won't take long before you know your way around..

available resources, which you should be able to identify using the Process tab (as detailed above).

You can click on the thumbnail graphs running down the left-hand side of the Task Manager to get more detail on each section. Even greater levels of detail – such as the demands being placed on each processor core – can be accessed by clicking Open Resource Monitor at the foot of the Task Manager window.

APP HISTORY App History is in many ways similar to Processes, detailing and heatmapping the demands of various applications. However, in this case it's restricted solely to the new Modern UI-style apps introduced with Windows 8, and as such includes a few extra details.

You will, for example, see listings for Network and Metered Network activity. The latter is particularly useful: it measures how much data an application is using while you're using a mobile data connection. As many mobile tariffs have strict data caps or charges per MB – especially when roaming on a foreign network – it's useful to know which apps are chomping through the most data, so you can shut them down or even uninstall them completely.

Also worth watching is the Tile updates column. This reveals if an app is clogging up system performance through the constant live updates that are an option for tiles on the new Windows Start screen. If it's gobbling up

too much memory, you can switch the live tile updates off by going to the Start screen, dragging the relevant app's tile upwards, and selecting "Turn Live Tile Off" from the options that appear at the foot of the screen.

START-UP The final tab of note in the new Task Manager is Start-up. This feature is a newcomer to the Task Manager, having previously been tucked away in the msconfig menu, where few casual users would ever have thought to look. This tab allows you to determine which programs are allowed to start up automatically every time you switch on or restart your PC.

More often than not, programs that embed themselves in the Start-up sequence are either critical (such as antivirus software) or harmless (such as Dropbox, or Microsoft's own SkyDrive) that run in the background waiting to be called into action. Some software, however, needlessly worms its way into the Start menu and merely adds to the time it takes to get your PC into a useful state after boot up. Usefully, the Start-up tab also provides an indication of the impact each program has on start-up time.

To stop a program loading each time you switch on your PC, highlight it in the list and click Disable. Make sure you know what you're switching off: if in doubt, it's best to leave it running, as other programs may depend on that app running in the background to function properly.

IN THIS CHAPTER

76 **Working with disc images** No DVD drive? No problem – Windows 8 can open disc images directly

78 **BitLocker** Use strong encryption to protect all your personal data and drives

80 **Advanced startup options** If Windows 8 won't boot, these troubleshooting options will help

82 **Secure Boot** This new security feature shuts out malware and closes off data leaks

84 **Windows To Go** Why carry a laptop? In Windows 8 you can transport your system on a USB stick

86 **Extend battery life** We show you how to keep Windows 8 laptops and tablets running longer

88 **Accessibility features** Make Windows easier to use with a screen reader, magnifier and more

5
Advanced features

ADVANCED FEA

Windows 8 is so straightforward to set up and use that you could easily overlook some of the more advanced features hidden away under the surface. BitLocker encryption, for instance, enables you to password-protect your documents and removable drives to ensure your precious data doesn't fall into the wrong hands. Or how about the revolutionary Windows To Go,

TURES

which gives business users the option of leaving their PC at home and only carrying around a simple USB flash drive containing their operating system and applications? In this chapter we'll look at these and other advanced Windows 8 features, including enhanced accessibility tools that ensure everybody can enjoy the new generation of computing equally.

Working with disk images

Windows 8 introduces powerful new capabilities for working with disk images – data files that store the complete contents of a physical hard disk. You may have come across disk images before in the ISO format, which is a popular way of archiving CDs and DVDs: many Linux distributions, for example, are offered in the form of downloadable ISO files.

The archived contents of an ISO file like this aren't able to be accessed directly. The file first has to be written directly to a blank CD or DVD, from which you can then boot to install the new operating system.

This method of distributing software is clever, but it's not always convenient. Many of today's laptops come without an optical drive, so once you've downloaded an ISO you may be left with no way of burning it to a disc. For this reason, some third-party developers have created software that lets you access the contents of an ISO directly – and in Windows 8 the ability is built in.

Looking inside an ISO file in Windows 8 is as simple as double-clicking it. The image will be loaded directly as a virtual drive, complete with its own drive letter, and you can browse the contents directly in Windows Explorer and in applications just as if it were a physical CD or DVD.

Mounting an ISO isn't a perfect alternative to using a real disc, as you can't boot from a mounted image – at least not without using some quite complex technical tools. But mounting is more convenient than burning, as you can check out the contents of an ISO without wasting a blank disc, and files can be read at the speed of your hard disk, rather than that of a much slower optical drive.

VIRTUAL HARD DISK FORMAT Another popular disk image type is the Virtual Hard Disk (VHD). This is similar to an ISO file, but instead of storing the contents of a CD or DVD, it instead serves as a regular hard disk in its own right. This means you can not only read its contents, but add to and change the files contained within the VHD.

VHDs are frequently used in virtualisation. If you're running Windows 8 Professional or Enterprise, you can install Microsoft's Hyper-V virtualisation host from the "Turn Windows features on or off" window – find it by searching in Settings. Once it's installed you can create a virtual PC within your regular Windows installation, with the VHD as its storage. If you ever need to access the files on your "real" Windows 8 system, you can simply double-click on the VHD to mount it as a virtual drive.

VHDs can also be created outside of Hyper-V. This can be convenient if, for example, you need to share a large set of files with someone else, in such a way that the contents are all stored in their proper places, but your colleague can still update and move things if needed.

Tip

If you need to create a bootable disc from an ISO but don't have a DVD burner, download the Microsoft Windows 7 USB DVD Download tool from www.pcpro.co.uk/links/win7tool. Despite the name this utility can be used to burn almost any ISO to a USB flash drive for easy booting.

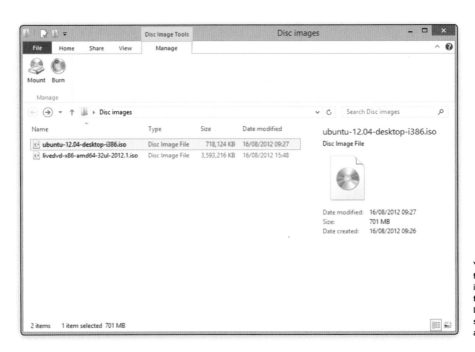

You may already be familiar with disc images in the ISO format, which is how Linux distributions such as Ubuntu are offered.

HOW TO...
HANDLE DISK IMAGES

(1) MOUNT THE IMAGE When you right-click on an ISO file, you'll see the default option is to Mount it. You can also burn an ISO directly from this menu, or from the Disc Image Tools tab in Explorer, so long as you have a DVD writer and a blank disc to hand. In most cases, however, you'll simply want to double-click to mount the image. Its contents will then appear in the Computer view just as if it were a real drive. You can browse the files and folders in Explorer and even share its contents with other users on your network.

(2) CHANGE DISC SETTINGS If for any reason you decide you want to change the drive letter of your mounted ISO, you can do so from the Disk Management console – look for the "Create and format hard disk partitions" option within the Control Panel to access it. You'll see your mounted ISO displayed just as if it were a real drive, and by right-clicking on it you can change various settings. You can't reformat the virtual disc, though: just like real CDs and DVDs mounted ISOs are read-only. If you want to edit files from an ISO, you'll have to copy them off onto your real hard disk first.

(3) EJECT THE VIRTUAL DRIVE When you've finished accessing the contents of an ISO, dismount it by selecting Eject, either from the Drive Tools tab in Explorer or from the drive's contextual menu in the Computer window. But you don't have to bother: the image will be dismounted automatically when you restart Windows. Bear this in mind if you want to share the contents of an ISO over a network, as it means your sharing settings will be lost when you reboot; there's no easy way to make virtual drive settings survive a reboot.

(4) CREATE YOUR OWN IMAGE You can also create disk images from the Disk Management console. Select Create VHD from the Action menu to create a new image of your chosen size. Once you've created your virtual disk it'll be automatically "attached" – that is, mounted – but you'll need to initialise it by right-clicking on its disk number in the console, then right-click on the disk graphic to create a new volume. Once this is done, the VHD will be available for you to use like a regular drive. If you want to move or rename the enclosing VHD file you'll have to "Eject" the virtual disk first.

HOW LONG?
The most common disk image operations can be carried out with a few clicks.

HOW HARD?
A little technical understanding is required to get the most from ISOs and VHDs.

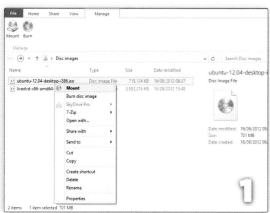

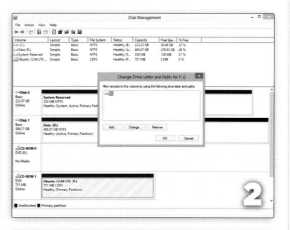

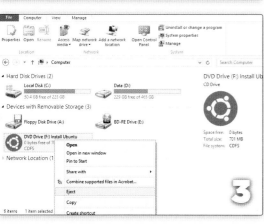

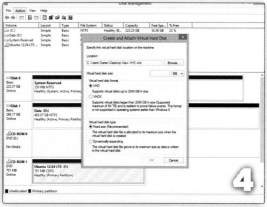

IF YOU WORK WITH CONFIDENTIAL OR SENSITIVE INFORMATION, BITLOCKER CAN ENSURE YOUR DATA DOESN'T FALL INTO THE WRONG HANDS

Protect your data with BitLocker

BitLocker is a data encryption system included in the Professional and Enterprise editions of Windows 8. Use it to protect the hard disk in your laptop, and even if the worst happens and your computer is stolen, the data stored on it will be inaccessible without your password.

Then there's BitLocker To Go, which can be used to encrypt removable hard disks and flash drives to keep your data safe even if the drive itself is stolen or misplaced.

BitLocker To Go is a godsend for anyone who regularly handles confidential data, and gives system administrators the option to stipulate that USB flash drives can only be used on company workstations if BitLocker encryption is enabled. That may sound strict, but it's a lot more lenient than banning USB drives altogether.

SETTING A PASSWORD BitLocker has plenty of depth: it can be teamed up with hardware security features to provide a united security front, for example, or coupled with a digital smart card for physical authentication. For most purposes, though, all you need to do is activate BitLocker on the drive you want to protect and enter a password.

It's worth putting a bit of thought into your password. If someone gets their hands on your hard disk, they'll have all the time they need to guess the password,

so make sure it's nothing easily guessable. One easy way to make a memorable but obscure password is to use a nonsensical phrase: "I made 11 biscuits and watched Columbo", for example, is unlikely to be high on most hackers' list of potential possibilities.

Don't pick a short password just because it's easy to type. What you can do, however, is configure a disk to automatically unlock whenever it's plugged into a trusted PC. That way at least you won't have to type it regularly.

Once you've entered a password, Windows will generate a recovery key: you can save this to your Microsoft Account or to a local text file, or print it out. The key itself is a 48-character string that can decrypt the drive on its own should you forget your password. This is your only way of ever getting your data back if you do lose your password, so keep it safely stored away, ideally in more than one place.

WORKING WITH OTHER OPERATING SYSTEMS Removable disks encrypted with BitLocker To Go can be accessed by all Windows 8 and Windows 7 PCs, so you should have no problem moving between computers. Connect it to a Windows XP or Vista system and you'll be given the option to install BitLocker To Go Reader, which can provide access to your files but won't let you modify or add to them.

Tip

To encrypt a single file or folder, right-click, select Properties, click Advanced... and tick "Encrypt contents to secure data". This encryption system doesn't use passwords: access is simply restricted to your user account alone. You can authorise other accounts too by clicking Details... in the Advanced Attributes window. The names of Encrypted files will appear in green in Windows Explorer.

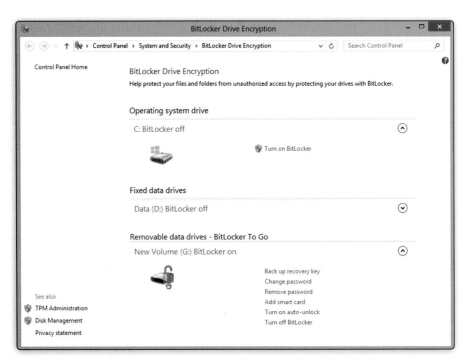

The Professional and Enterprise versions of Windows 8 offer BitLocker encryption tools to protect your hard disk from unwanted attention, while BitLocker To Go does the same job for removable drives.

HOW TO...
SET UP BITLOCKER

 1 **ENCRYPT THE DISK** To encrypt a disk, select it in the Computer view in Explorer, go to the Drive Tools tab and select Turn on BitLocker from the drop-down. If you want to encrypt your system disk, your computer will need a TPM (Trusted Platform Module) chip. However, other drives can be freely encrypted with no special hardware requirements. You'll be prompted to select a password and/or insert a smart card with which to secure the disk. If you don't have a smart card (most of us don't), leave this option unticked and just enter a suitably unguessable password.

2 **STORE A RECOVERY KEY** You'll then be prompted to store your recovery key. This key is in effect a universal key that can completely unlock your data, so keep it safe, just as you'd protect your actual password. Next you'll be asked exactly how much of the disk you want to encrypt. Be aware that encrypting the full capacity of a large hard disk can take hours. That said, encrypt only the used space and it's possible that files that were previously stored on the disk could still be retrieved, We recommend you use this option only if the disk you want to encrypt is brand new, or you're sure has never previously been used to store confidential information.

 3 **READING A BITLOCKER DISK** Accessing a disk encrypted with BitLocker is easy. If it's your system disk, you'll be prompted to provide the BitLocker password (or other credentials as configured by you) before the system can boot. Other BitLocker volumes will appear in the Computer view with a padlock icon, and if you plug in an encrypted removable drive a tile will appear on the desktop telling you the disk needs unlocking. Click on the tile and a password requester will appear, inviting you to enter the password you have chosen for your encrypted volume. Once this is done the disk can be used as normal.

 4 **RECOVER FROM A LOST PASSWORD** Should you forget your BitLocker password, click More Options and enter your 48-character recovery key. You'll also notice the "Automatically unlock on this PC" option, which allows you to side-step the need for a password altogether on PCs you trust. This feature can be turned off again from the BitLocker Drive Encryption window in the Control Panel. You can change your password here, remove it completely (if you'd prefer smart card authentication only) or turn off BitLocker encryption altogether.

HOW LONG?
Depending on how full your hard disk is, encryption can take quite a long time.

HOW HARD?
Encryption is a complex topic, but Windows 8 makes it as simple as is possible.

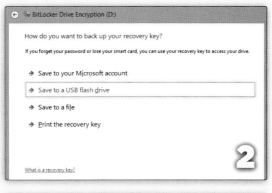

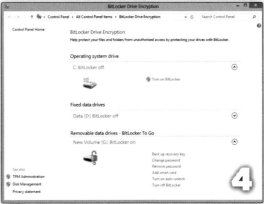

 IF WINDOWS 8 STOPS WORKING, DON'T PANIC: THE OS INCLUDES PLENTY OF BUILT-IN OPTIONS AND TOOLS TO HELP YOU RECOVER YOUR SYSTEM

Advanced startup options

When you turn on your PC, Windows normally boots up to the familiar login screen and everything is as it should be. But what if something goes wrong and Windows can't start? In previous editions of Windows you might end up stuck in an endless cycle of reboots, or be dumped into a daunting screen full of black and grey text.

In Windows 8, you'll be pleased to hear, things are much friendlier. If Windows 8 fails to start up correctly twice in a row, the third attempt will take you to a graphical interface that can be controlled by mouse, keyboard or touch. The first screen you'll see will warn you that "it looks like Windows didn't load correctly". If you want to try rebooting, you can do that from here; otherwise, click "See advanced repair options" and you'll be taken to Windows 8's advanced startup options.

REFRESHING AND RESETTING YOUR PC The next screen that appears offers you a couple of options. The bottom one – Turn off your PC – speaks for itself; the top one, Continue, lets you try once more to boot Windows 8, on the off chance that you might have changed your mind in the past few seconds.

If you have a bootable external hard disk or CD installed, the second option you'll see may be Use a device,

which enables you to boot from another drive. If you have more than one operating system installed on your hard disk, the next option in the list down will be to Use another operating system – to boot, for example, into your old Windows 7 system.

The penultimate option, labelled Troubleshoot, is where things start to get interesting. Clicking on this takes you through to another set of three options – Refresh your PC, Reset your PC and Advanced options. The first two represent pretty major software surgery: Refresh reinstalls the operating system, saving your data and Modern apps, but removing all desktop applications. The latter option, Reset your PC, is even more drastic: it completely reverts your PC to its just-installed state. We cover these options in more detail in Chapter 8.

If you're daunted by the prospect of either of these options, a click of the back arrow next to the title will take you back to the previous screen. Click Advanced options, however, and you'll see another page of options that allow you to delve even deeper into the operating system's innards – this includes tools that might enable you to get Windows up and running again without you having to say goodbye to your programs or settings.

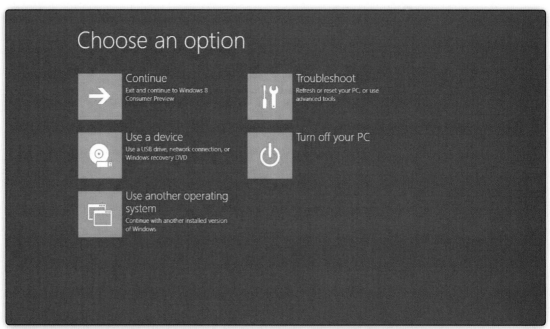

Your options for dealing with startup issues in Windows 8 are presented in far more friendly terms than in the past.

> **Tip**
>
> A few advanced boot features – such as "Use a device" – rely on modern hardware features. If you install Windows 8 on an older PC, the menu will still work, but if you want to boot from a USB flash drive or a DVD you'll have to configure this in the BIOS.

The PC settings menu contains a range of troubleshooting options to address startup issues or simply improve PC performance.

HOW LONG?
There are plenty of tools to try out: some are quick, others decidedly slower.

HOW HARD?
Some recovery options require a technical understanding.

ADVANCED OPTIONS The Advanced options page is a good first stop any time you're having trouble getting Windows working properly. You might initially wonder why it's tucked away so deeply in the system, but the tools here aren't for novices. The top option is System Restore: this will boot Windows into a stripped-down desktop, from which you can selectively undo recent installations and settings changes. For more on System Restore, see Chapter 8.

The next option is System Image Recovery. This reverts your hard disk to a previous state, using a system image file created by the built-in (but misleadingly named) Windows 7 File Recovery tool. If you haven't created such an image in advance, though, this option can't help you. Even if you do have an image to restore from, consider it a last resort, as any documents created or edited since then will be overwritten and lost.

The third option is Automatic Repair: this fixes problems caused by, for example, adding or removing hard disks, which can cause Windows to look in the wrong place for files. It takes only a minute to run, but if you haven't changed your hardware it's unlikely to cure your problem.

Option four is to open a Command Prompt: if you're a technically experienced Windows user you can run your own diagnostics from here, and even use disk partitioning and repair tools if need be. Again, though, if Windows has stopped working abruptly it's unlikely that the problem lies at this sort of low level – it's much more likely to be a flaky program or device driver – so don't worry if the Command Prompt is beyond you.

The final option is Windows Startup Settings. From here you can reboot to a special menu that allows you to enable and disable various system settings. You can try to boot Windows in Safe Mode, a special operating mode in which most programs and drivers aren't loaded, giving you a chance to change settings and remove or update software, to see if this fixes your problem. Alternatively, you can specify low-resolution video mode, to help troubleshoot problems with display drivers.

ACCESSING ADVANCED STARTUP OPTIONS Some of Windows 8's advanced boot options are useful even if your computer isn't having trouble starting up. The option to "Use another operating system", for example, allows you to choose which OS will boot by default each time you restart your PC. Starting up in Safe Mode or low-resolution video mode might help you track down intermittent problems.

You might also want to boot into a special mode called "Disable driver signature enforcement", which lets you install older drivers that aren't digitally signed by their publishers. Windows 8 normally blocks them as a potential security risk, but if you need to use an older unsigned driver to get a device working, this mode will let you do it.

To access the advanced startup options from within Windows, simply search Settings for "advanced startup". You'll find the relevant button on the main Windows 8 PC Settings screen, at the bottom of the General section. Click it and Windows will restart, booting into the advanced options interface.

 DON'T BELIEVE THE SCARE STORIES: SECURE BOOT IS A POWERFUL SYSTEM THAT PUTS YOU IN CONTROL OF YOUR PC'S SECURITY

Staying safe with Secure Boot

One of the more controversial features introduced with Windows 8 is Secure Boot. Going on the name alone you'd be forgiven for thinking this is a good thing, and in practice it is. However, when the feature was first announced, not everyone understood exactly what it does and how it works. There were concerns that it might cause every Windows 8 PC to be "locked" to that operating system, preventing you from installing competing systems such as Ubuntu Linux. In fact, this fear is a long way from the truth. Let's take a look at exactly what Secure Boot is, why it's a good thing – and why those fears are unfounded.

WHAT SECURE BOOT DOES Simply put, Secure Boot ensures that only authorised operating systems are able to start up on your PC. Ordinarily, when you switch your computer on, the BIOS goes through a few checks, such as briefly testing the memory modules and checking that all available disk drives are present and working correctly, then hands over

control to the bootloader – the little piece of code on the hard disk which loads the full operating system.

Secure Boot adds an extra step to this process: before handing over control, it reads a digital signature embedded in the bootloader and verifies it against an internal database. All new PCs and laptops that come with a Windows 8 sticker will have Microsoft's certificate pre-installed in this database, so Windows 8 will start up without complaint. If the bootloader has a different signature – that is, if it's a different operating system – the system will refuse to boot.

It's easy to see why some people were alarmed when Secure Boot was first described. On the face of it, it sounds like new PCs running Windows 8 will be locked to that one operating system forever.

But it's important to realise that if you don't like Secure Boot you can simply turn it off. There are good reasons to leave it activated, which we'll go into shortly.

But if you do want to experiment with operating systems other than Windows 8, simply disable Secure Boot from the BIOS interface and carry on just as before.

A second key point is that any bootloader can be authorised. Already, the publishers of Fedora Linux have struck a deal with Microsoft which means their Linux distribution will be automatically approved by Windows 8 Secure Boot systems.

And even if you do decide to use a system that isn't supported directly, you can add your own certificates to your computer's Secure Boot database. For example, if you have two hard disks in a desktop system you might want to install Ubuntu on the second one. Simply add a certificate for Ubuntu to your BIOS and you'll be able to boot natively from either disk, with other bootloaders remaining blacklisted. The precise process for generating a Secure Boot key should be detailed in the manual for your motherboard or laptop, or in the installation instructions for the operating system.

For maximum security, it's also possible to delete certificates. For example, if you want to wipe Windows 8 from your new PC you can remove its key from the database, preventing anyone from booting into that OS.

THE ADVANTAGES OF SECURE BOOT At this point you're probably wondering: why would I want to prevent certain operating systems from loading up on my PC? There are two good answers to this. The first one is that it helps businesses enforce their security policies. Many companies have strict rules on what software can be run, what sort of network access is permitted and so forth. If users are able to plug in their own hard disks and boot into unauthorised operating systems, however, those security measures could easily be

bypassed, raising the possibility of a data leak, a virus attack or even corporate espionage.

Secure Boot provides peace of mind against these eventualities. All the IT department has to do is enable the feature and protect the BIOS of each client PC with a password, to prevent meddling users from disabling it. Immediately the potential data leak is closed.

What about home users? Here, too, Secure Boot can protect your security. In this scenario, the risk isn't from corporate spies, however: but rather from malware. Specifically, Secure Boot protects you against a nasty type of infection called a "rootkit" that works by infecting the bootloader of the operating system, installing its own code before the rest of Windows is loaded into memory.

This approach allows a functioning rootkit to change Windows settings, steal data and do whatever else it likes without being detected. Secure Boot stops rootkits in their tracks, because as soon as the bootloader is tampered with, its digital signature will change and the computer will refuse to load it.

SECURE BOOT ON WINDOWS RT By now it should be clear that when it comes to Windows 8 desktops and laptops, Secure Boot doesn't shut you out of anything: it simply sets a baseline of security which you are free to adjust.

There is, however, one important exception to this rule. If you buy an ARM-based Windows 8 device running Windows RT, you won't be able to disable Secure Boot. Microsoft wants Windows 8 tablets to provide a completely consistent experience, with no possibility of malware or confusing multiple environments, so Secure Boot is locked and all third-party bootloaders are strictly banned. It's Windows 8 or nothing.

HOW LONG?
Tweaking your settings involves a little delving into the BIOS.

HOW HARD?
Secure Boot keeps to itself, working behind the scenes to keep you safe.

Secure Boot prevents rogue rootkits from infiltrating your PC.

WANT TO TAKE YOUR PC WITH YOU? WINDOWS 8'S NEW WINDOWS TO GO FEATURE LETS YOU USE ANY PC AS IF IT WERE YOUR OWN

Windows To Go

Have you ever found yourself away from home – perhaps on holiday, or a business trip – and wished you had access to your work PC? Alternatively, wouldn't it be great if you could take your own hardware into the office and use it for work, without fear of screwing up all your personal network and application settings? Well, with the new Windows To Go feature in Windows 8 you can – or at least you can under certain circumstances.

INTRODUCING WINDOWS TO GO Windows To Go is a clever system that enables you to install Windows and your applications directly onto a USB flash drive. You can then boot from this drive on whatever PC hardware you like and have instant access to whatever programs and settings you've installed.

It's a versatile system that has several useful applications. For executives, carrying around a USB stick is far more convenient than having to lug a laptop around with you everywhere you go – and if disaster does strike the cost of replacing a lost or stolen USB stick is several orders of magnitude lower than what it will cost to replace a whole laptop – never mind the information on it.

The USB drive can be encrypted with BitLocker (see p78), so the data on it will be completely inaccessible to anyone who finds it. In short, so long as there's a computer you can use when you get where you're going, Windows To Go is a godsend for travellers.

Windows To Go is equally well suited to hotdesking. It enables companies to provide a certain number of standard PCs at its offices that anyone can use to boot into their personal Windows 8 environment without fear of compromising the security of the greater network.

TECHNICAL REQUIREMENTS Windows To Go is only available in the Enterprise edition of Windows 8. If you have this edition, you can very easily create your own portable Windows 8 system by running the Windows To Go Creator wizard. If you have the regular domestic or Professional edition, however, you're out of luck.

For those who can use it, Windows To Go is impressively unfussy. Officially, only a small number of USB flash drives are supported, but in practice we've found the system works with all sorts of devices, including regular external hard disks.

Tip

To boot from a Windows To Go drive, you might need to go into your PC's BIOS settings and give the USB drive a higher priority than the local hard disk. In Windows 8 you can also specify that the PC should always boot from a Windows To Go drive if one is plugged in: to access this setting, search Settings for "Windows To Go Startup Options".

Windows To Go effectively lets you carry around your entire PC on a single USB drive.

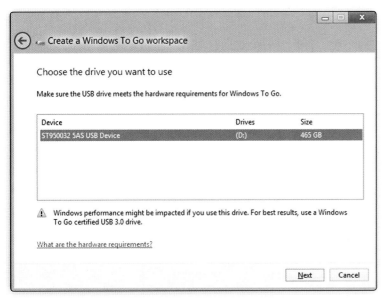

Windows To Go prefers a USB 3 connection, but it's by no means compulsory, and the system will remember the configuration of every PC you plug it into, so you have to set it up only once.

HOW LONG?
It takes a while to create the Windows To Go system at first.

HOW HARD?
It's easy, but there are some caveats to bear in mind.

Microsoft also specifies that a USB 3 connection should be used in order to make sure things keep running smoothly. Again, though, we've found Windows To Go is perfectly slick and usable over a USB 2 connection.

One area where it is worth paying attention to Microsoft's technical stipulations, however, is when it comes to the free storage space needed on your USB flash drive. At least 20GB of space is recommended, which obviously means you're looking at a 32GB drive at the very least. It may technically be possible to squeeze a stripped-down Windows 8 installation onto a 16GB drive if you have no other choice, but be aware that space for documents and applications will be very tight indeed.

USING WINDOWS TO GO For the most part, using Windows To Go feels just like using a regular Windows 8 PC. When you boot on a computer you haven't previously used, Windows To Go will automatically install all the necessary drivers for that particular hardware setup onto the USB stick, so you can expect full support for graphics hardware, touchscreens and more. The installation process does take a minute or two to complete, but it's well worth the trouble, as it means Windows 8 will remember that PC in the future, so the next time you boot on it the drivers will be preconfigured and ready to go.

Once you're in, you'll find there are only a handful of things that Windows To Go can't do. One of these is hibernate, and the reason is that it prevents you from accidentally suspending the system on one computer then resuming it on another, which could cause instability. The Windows Store is also disabled by default, since downloaded apps are linked to specific hardware, so installing a Windows 8 app on a Windows To Go system could cause confusion.

It's worth noting too that while you're using Windows To Go, the computer's local hard disk is automatically set offline: this ensures you can't possibly leave behind any traces of what you've been doing. Similarly, if you plug a Windows To Go drive into a PC that's already running Windows, it won't show up in the Computer view. This makes it impossible for any malware or spying software that may have got onto the host PC to find its way onto your Windows To Go system, or vice versa. If you want, though, you can easily mount a disk that's been set offline and copy files back and forth, so long as they're not encrypted.

What happens if you accidentally pull the USB drive out of its socket? On a regular Windows installation disconnecting the system disk would cause the OS to crash immediately, but Windows To Go is more robust: if you plug the drive back in within a minute, you can simply continue working as if nothing had happened. After a minute the system will shut down, clearing memory and erasing any trace of what you were doing on that PC.

Although Windows To Go is a brand-new system, it has been well thought through, and should prove highly useful to those in a position to take advantage of it. We have one caveat, though: when you're working on a "To Go" workstation, any changes you make to your files won't be synchronised automatically back to your original PC, so you could end up with multiple versions of documents. We recommend you use a cloud syncing service such as SkyDrive (see Chapter 7) to keep everything in step.

Extend your battery life

Windows 8 is designed to be used on the go – on laptops, tablets and all those clever hybrid devices that lie in between. Naturally, therefore, you'll want to do whatever you can to extend its battery life.

If you've used Windows 7 or Vista on a laptop before, you'll be right at home with Windows 8, as it uses the same system of "power plans" – operating modes that balance performance against speed. The easiest way to access these plans is to search Settings for Power Options and click on the icon that comes up.

In the window that opens, you'll be given a simple choice. It's possible that the manufacturer of your laptop or tablet will have preconfigured custom power settings; by default, though, Windows 8 uses the built-in Balanced power plan. This allows the CPU to run at full pelt when it's needed, dropping to a low level of power consumption when it isn't being pushed. With this plan active, if you spend your time browsing the web or typing up word processing documents, your battery should last for several hours, while games and heavy number-crunching tasks will exhaust the power much more quickly.

If battery life is paramount, you can click to activate the Power Saver plan instead. As soon as you do this, your screen is dimmed, the processor is reined in and other unnecessary services are halted to help your battery

last longer. There's a third option too, although it's hidden away: click the arrow next to "Show additional plans" and you'll see the High Performance plan. This lets all the components in your system run at full speed, regardless of power usage.

Once you've set a power plan, you don't have to stick with it. To switch between plans, simply click on the battery symbol at the bottom right of the Taskbar. You'll initially be presented with the two most recently used choices. Clicking "More power options" opens the full Power Options window.

TWEAKING SETTINGS The default power plans are fine for everyday computing, but there's more control on offer if you want it. You'll see additional options in the left-hand pane of the Power Options window, including an opportunity to create your own bespoke power plan.

You can also customise one of the pre-installed power plans, by clicking its "Change plan settings" link. This shows more settings, allowing you to specify when, under the selected plan, the display will be switched off and when the computer will go into Sleep mode. You can specify a default screen brightness too: a screen running at full brightness is one of the most power-hungry components of a typical laptop, so turning this down a few notches can

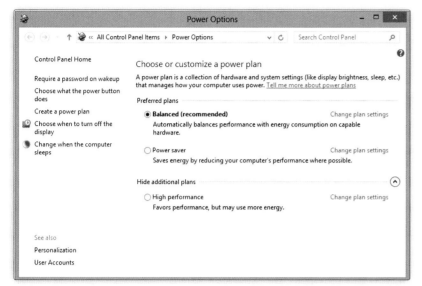

For tablet users in particular, the range of power management tools in Windows 8 is a major plus.

There are three global power management settings, but each can be fine-tuned to suit your needs.

HOW LONG?
Picking a power plan takes mere moments.

HOW HARD?
There are a few technical issues to consider, but it's largely simple stuff.

make a surprising difference to your battery life. If you find you occasionally want things brighter, almost all laptops have shortcut buttons on the keyboard to temporarily raise and lower brightness.

If you want to get even more hands-on, click "Change advanced power settings" to open up a new world of tweakery. From the window that opens you can control all sorts of variables: for example, you can turn off your hard disk after a certain period of inactivity, or selectively suspend USB ports that aren't being used to stop them draining a trickle of power. You can also tweak your processor, specifying minimum and maximum levels of CPU activity, so that when you don't need all of your system's capability you can throttle down the chip to prevent it draining excessive battery power.

Many of these options can be set to different levels depending on whether your laptop is plugged in or running on the battery, so there's no need to limit your computer's performance when you're on the mains.

DISABLE UNWANTED FEATURES An additional way to conserve a bit of battery power is to deactivate power-hungry programs and components. Unneeded startup items keep your CPU busy and your disks spinning, wasting charge: such programs can be switched off from the Task Manager, as described in Chapter 4.

The wireless transmitters and receivers inside your laptop also draw plenty of power, and if you're not online, they're effectively sitting there draining the battery. Most laptops include a hardware switch or key combination for turning Wi-Fi on and off when it's not in use. Alternatively, you can achieve a similar result by putting Windows 8 into a no-network "airplane mode" by activating the Charms, selecting Settings, clicking on your network connection and activating the Airplane mode at the top of the screen.

To disable a device for the long term, you'll need to use the Device Manager. To find it, simply

search for "device manager" while in Settings. When the window opens, you'll see a whole hierarchy of connected devices. To disable one, right-click on its icon and select Disable. When you need to use it, just go back and enable it again.

SPRING CLEANING If you've installed Windows 8 on an older laptop, its internal cooling systems may no longer be in top condition: this will have a knock-on effect on your battery life, as a dusty PC will need to drive its fan harder because of the hotter, more claustrophobic conditions created inside its case.

If you're feeling brave, you can often unscrew the bottom of your machine to improve airflow to the fan that keeps your processor cool, while some further careful screw removal will let you pry the fan itself away from its mounting. Doing so will allow you to gently clean dust away from the fan and its vents (usually on the side of the machine), which will improve your computer's efficiency and make it consume less power.

 THE ACCESSIBILITY FEATURES IN WINDOWS 8 CAN HELP THE PARTIALLY
SIGHTED OR MOVEMENT IMPAIRED TO GET THE BEST FROM THEIR PC OR TABLET

Accessibility features

Computers aren't just for those lucky enough to have perfect vision and motor control. Computing is for everyone – and Windows 8 acknowledges that by offering more accessibility features than ever, ensuring that even those with visual or other impairments can run apps, go online and enjoy computing.

It all starts with Windows 8's Modern interface. Full-screen apps with big, clear text are a huge help for those who have difficulty reading small text, and if you have difficulty controlling a mouse or keyboard then a touchscreen interface could be just what's called for. Where appropriate, Windows 8 app developers are encouraged to mark their apps as accessible in the Windows Store, to help users identify the software that's most friendly to those with disabilities. It's a shame this information is hidden away under the Details tab of each app in the Windows Store, but it's a positive step.

Microsoft has also beefed up the accessibility features that we saw in Windows 7. A lot of work has gone into upgrading the Narrator function, which reads out the contents of windows and web pages to assist partially sighted users. If you've used this feature before, you'll find it faster and more accurate than previous versions. It works with new-style Modern UI apps downloaded from the Store too, and has been enhanced for touch-only devices. When Narrator is enabled on a Windows 8 tablet, you can simply drag a finger around the interface to hear Windows read out the text of each tile as you pass over it. When you find the item you want, tap with a second finger to select it.

Another pillar of Windows' accessibility features is the Magnifier, which lets you zoom in on individual screen elements. This, too, has been updated for touch interfaces: now you can drag the viewport around by dragging the edges of the screen, and if you tap two opposing borders you can temporarily zoom out to see where exactly you are on screen. Taken together, these enhancements make Windows 8 Microsoft's most accessible operating system yet.

DESKTOP SETTINGS Alongside these enhanced tools, Windows 8 retains all the familiar accessibility features of previous versions of the operating system. You'll find these in the Ease of Access Center in the Control Panel – a one-stop window providing instant access to Windows' accessibility features, and guidance to users who may not know which tools and options can help them.

At the very top of the window you'll see hard-to-miss links to the most commonly used accessibility features – but if you're not au fait with Windows' various accessibility options, the best place to start is by clicking "Get recommendations to make your computer easier to use". Click this and you'll be asked five questions relating to your eyesight, dexterity, hearing, speech and reasoning (for example, whether you find it difficult to concentrate or remember). On the basis of your answers, Windows will

Tip

◢ On tablet hardware, you can turn on Narrator by holding down the Windows key and pressing Volume Up. You can change this, however: in the Ease of Access Center, click "Make touch and tablets easier to use". You can now assign this button combination to launch the Magnifier or on-screen keyboard instead.

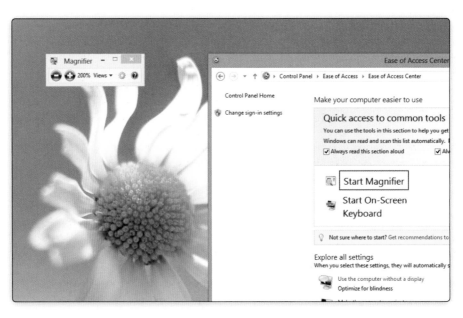

Windows' accessibility tools are better than ever in Windows 8, including useful options for users with impaired vision.

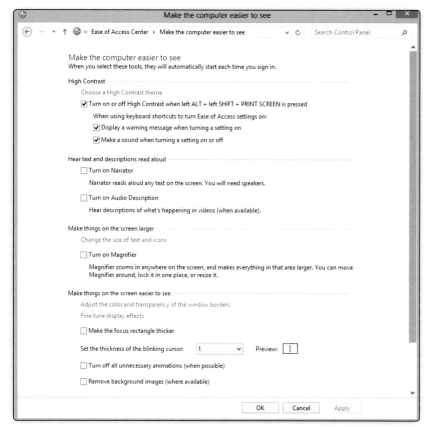

Microsoft has sensibly grouped the vast range of accessibility options under the goal they help to accomplish, such as "Make the computer easier to see".

HOW LONG?
Browse the options, then activate the ones you want with a click or a tap.

HOW HARD?
Accessibility settings are all clearly set out and easy to access.

suggest settings you might wish to change. Alternatively, scroll down the window and you can choose the settings manually, with each option clearly describing the goal it helps to achieve, such as "Make the computer easier to see" or "Make the keyboard easier to use".

SOUND AND VISION For those with visual impairments, Windows 8 offers several useful options. Some are minor but effective, such as enlarging the size of text and icons. Others include switching to the simplified white-on-black High Contrast theme and turning on the Magnifier.

For those with hearing difficulties, the "Get visual indications for sound" option replaces alerts and beeps with visual equivalents, such as a flashing caption bar or window, and you can choose to have spoken dialogue converted into text captions.

There's also help for those who have trouble using a keyboard or mouse. Along with options such as Sticky Keys – allowing you to press keystroke combinations in sequence rather than simultaneously – Windows 8 offers keyboard and mouse filters designed to intelligently assist your movements and keep rogue clicks and presses to a minimum. An on-screen keyboard lets you use a mouse to enter text; conversely, a feature called MouseKeys lets you use the arrows on your numeric keypad to guide the mouse pointer around. Whichever way you want to use Windows, it's supported in Windows 8.

There's even a speech control and recognition system, built on the principle of "say what you see". With this switched on, speak the name of a button or menu item and it should be selected. If that fails, say "show numbers", and Windows covers active areas of the current window with numbers. State the number of your chosen option, and Windows will activate that button or link. The system requires a certain amount of training, but Windows 8 makes the process relatively quick and easy through a series of tutorial and training exercises that give you a chance to learn the system at the same time as it's learning to recognise your voice.

Finally, anyone with difficulty concentrating will appreciate a selection of options aimed at minimising distractions. You can disable or limit window animations, and prevent windows from snapping or rearranging themselves at the edges of the screen, to ensure more predictable behaviour of on-screen elements.

ACCESSIBLE LOGON Accessibility features that only kick in when you get to the desktop aren't much use if you can't get to the desktop in the first place. Click "Change sign-in settings" in the Ease of Access Center window and you'll see a list of accessibility options that can be enabled on the login screen, including Narrator, Magnifier and Sticky Keys. You can also click the accessibility icon at the bottom left of the login screen to enable these features on a one-off basis.

IN THIS CHAPTER

92 Introducing Internet Explorer 10

Microsoft's browser is faster than ever, and supports the latest exciting interactive web technologies.

94 Setting up a wireless network

Enjoy wireless internet in safety, whether at home, in the office, or out in the big wide world.

96 HomeGroup

HomeGroup makes it easy to share pictures, music, documents and even printers over your home network.

98 Using 3G on tablets

This is the first version of Windows built for tablets, so find out how you can access the internet via a built-in 3G connection.

6
Internet & networking

INTERNET AND

We're now in a connected world, where tablets are used to browse the internet as much as the PC or laptop. Windows 8 caters for all users, so in this chapter we'll show you how to get up and running online – both on the internet and on your home network. However you use Windows, you'll need a web browser, so we start with a look at Microsoft's new Internet Explorer 10 – in

NETWORKING

both touch and desktop versions. We'll explain how to set up a wireless network at home, and connect your PC or tablet to it with maximum speed and security. We'll examine the HomeGroup features for easily sharing files across multiple PCs, and reveal how you can use 3G to get online on your new Windows 8 tablet when you're out and about.

MICROSOFT'S WEB BROWSER ISN'T YOUR ONLY CHOICE, BUT ITS LATEST
INCARNATION HAS SOME NEAT TOUCHES, MAKING IT A GREAT STARTING POINT.

Introducing Internet Explorer 10

Although there are other popular browsers favoured by
Windows users – Mozilla Firefox and Google Chrome are
two of the better-known examples – Windows 8 introduces
Internet Explorer 10 to the world: an up-to-date, fully
featured web browser that works in both tablet and normal
desktop mode. Here we take a look at how it works on
whatever kind of device you're using, and what features
it offers to make it stand out from its browser rivals.

THE LOOK On the desktop, IE10 works much like any other
browser, but is sensibly designed to be as unobtrusive as
possible, so as not to distract from your favourite sites.
Along the top you'll see an address bar, where – as always
– you can type or paste in web addresses. If you type
something that isn't a valid web address, IE10 will carry out
a web search instead. If you don't know the address of a taxi
firm in South London, for example, just type "south London
taxi" into the address bar and IE10 will display search results
for that phrase from Microsoft's Bing search engine. As you
type, IE10 will also display a live drop-down containing the
titles of any pages you've previously visited that contain
your phrase: just click on a title to jump to that specific page.

TABBED BROWSING Tabbed browsing enables you to have
multiple web pages open simultaneously within one browser
window. Hold down Ctrl and press T to open a new tab
without losing your original web page, or just click the
mini-tab visible to the right of the last open tab.

You can get Windows 8 to open any link you click
on in a new tab either by holding down Ctrl as you click
it, by right-clicking and selecting Open in new tab, or by
pressing the wheel of your mouse when hovering over the
link. The currently live tab will always be highlighted in the
bar, and you can switch between open tabs as often as you
like without any of them closing.

TOUCHSCREEN EXPLORER For the first time, Internet
Explorer is also designed to work as a touchscreen app
on a tablet, and in full-screen mode it's a very different
experience. Gone are the address bar and tabs, at least in the
traditional sense. It may look as though your web page now
has no controls for you to navigate with, but swipe inwards
from the top of your tablet's screen and they'll swish into
view: open tabs at the top, a larger, touch-friendly address
and search bar at the bottom.

Tap the plus icon to open a new tab, tap the
ellipses (…) for options, and use the controls by the address
bar for settings and pinned sites. If using a touchscreen-only
device such as a tablet, simply tap on the address bar and
a software keyboard will pop up on-screen, and results will
appear on the fly in the space above as you type. Just tap
one with a finger to open it.

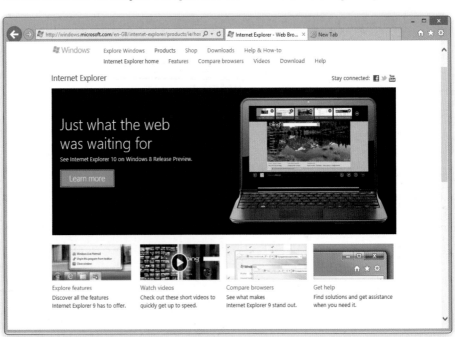

The interface of the
desktop version of
IE10 is designed to
be as unobtrusive
as possible, showing
only the web
address bar, your
open tabs and a few
key icons.

Tip

If you're browsing the
web on a tablet and
visit a site that is also
available in Modern
UI app form, you can
now download the app
automatically from
Internet Explorer. When
you're on a compatible
site, swipe from the
top edge to bring up
the menu, then tap the
Tools button. If an app
is available, you'll see
the option to "Get app
for this site". Tap that,
the app will download
and you won't need the
browser to view that
site from now on.

HOW TO...
USE IE10'S ADVANCED FEATURES

① MOST POPULAR SITES Internet Explorer 10 keeps track of the sites you visit, so that the next time you start the program or open a new tab, you can return to your favourite pages right away. Your grid of most frequently visited sites is automatically updated as you browse, with an activity monitor below each entry showing how frequently the site is updated, so you can see whether it's worth checking back. If there's a site you don't want to appear as a suggestion when you open a new tab, click the close icon at the top-right of its pane, and it'll be gone for good. In the touchscreen-enhanced Modern UI version of IE10, you can see this grid of most-visited sites by swiping up from the bottom of the screen.

② INPRIVATE BROWSING Beneath the grid of your most frequently visited pages, you'll find the InPrivate Browsing option (or swipe down from the top on a touchscreen and tap the ellipsis (...) button). In this mode, nothing you do online is logged on your system – useful if you have an online banking account, for example, and want to be sure your personal details won't be left behind on your PC. If you visit a web page in InPrivate Browsing mode, it won't appear in your internet history, and no cookies will be kept on your system. However, be aware that this doesn't make you totally anonymous: the websites themselves can still keep track of you, as can your home ISP or your office network.

③ FLIP AHEAD When displaying a long article, many sites will break up the pages so at first glance it doesn't seem such a daunting read. IE10 detects these multi-page articles and preloads all the pages to save you waiting for each one to load. Assuming the browser correctly detects that you're reading a long article, you should be able to click or tap the Forward button at the top of the first page to "flip ahead" to the next page without having to wait for it to load. The Forward button remains clickable until the last page of the article is reached. Turn on Flip Ahead in the Options menu.

④ PINNED SITES We've already seen how your most frequently visited sites are recorded and offered to you when you open a new tab, but the new version of Internet Explorer also lets you pin your favourite sites directly into the Start screen of Windows 8 for one-click access. Just navigate to a site you like, and swipe up from the bottom of the screen to bring up the Pinned menu. Tap the pin icon in the bottom-right and select "Pin to Start", then give your shortcut a suitable name. And that's it. Once done, if you press the home button to bring up your Start screen, you should see the new shortcut to your saved site among the usual grid of icons, and hopefully the system should pull in its icon to use as the Windows 8 tile. Whenever you want to visit that site, just click the icon to open IE and head straight to it.

HOW LONG?
Internet Explorer 10 comes pre-installed. Just click on the icon to get started.

HOW HARD?
The basics are very intuitive, but if you want to make the most of IE10, there are a few controls and shortcuts to master.

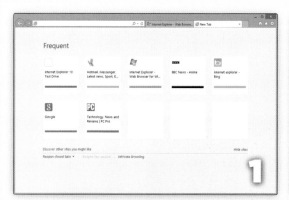

WINDOWS 8 IS DESIGNED TO WORK SEAMLESSLY WITH WIRELESS NETWORKS, MAKING IT EASY TO SET UP A HOME ROUTER AND CONNECT YOUR PC

Setting up a wireless network

Broadband internet is now almost ubiquitous, so there's a good chance you already have a wireless router in your home. If not, this is certainly as good a time as any to change that and embrace the freedom of wireless internet accessible anywhere in the home.

Assuming you do own a router, however, it's worth making sure it's configured to give you optimum performance and security. The specifics of setting up a router vary from model to model: you'll need to check the manufacturer's instructions for precise details on how to connect to the router from your PC and change its settings.

In general, though, you can usually log in by typing the router's IP address (http://192.168.1.1, for example) into your browser. Search online using your router's make and model to confirm its IP address if you're not sure.

CHOOSE A PASSWORD Logging into your router will require an Administrator password – by default it will be set to a disturbingly predictable preset (either "admin" or nothing at all are two favourites) that is listed in the manual. Change this as soon as possible. Standard passwords are common knowledge among hackers, and you don't want strangers to be able to change your settings.

CHOOSE AN SSID The SSID (Serve Set Identifier) is the name your wireless network shows to the world. Change the default name (it will be something like "Default Network" or the name of your router's manufacturer) to clearly identify the router as your own, but avoid using your name or address as this could make life easier for tech-savvy thieves.

SET UP SECURITY To avoid strangers being able to connect to your network, your router will offer various security systems. Your best bet is WPA2-PSK (your router may call it WPA2 Personal, or just WPA2). It's very secure and works with smartphones and tablets, Wi-Fi printers, games consoles and other wireless devices. If some of your kit doesn't support WPA2, standard WPA should still deter casual hackers, but WEP is best avoided if you can help it.

Once you enable WPA2, you'll be asked to choose a password. It should be more than eight characters long; it should be memorable to you, but impossible to guess.

PICK A PROTOCOL Ensure your router is set up to use the fastest Wi-Fi protocol your PC supports (*see Tip, left*). This may not speed up web browsing, but a higher protocol can help speed up file transfers and improve Wi-Fi reception too.

Tip

Wireless networking uses five protocols – all referred to as "802.11" followed by a letter. 802.11a was designed for business and isn't commonly used in the home. Of the commonly used protocols, 802.11b is slower than 802.11g, while 802.11n is even faster than 802.11g. There's a new, even faster standard emerging called 802.11ac, but there are very few compatible devices available at the time of writing.

Every router's setup page will differ depending on the manufacturer, but in many cases it'll be found at the address http://192.168.1.1.

HOW TO...
CONNECT TO A WI-FI NETWORK

(1) DURING INSTALLATION If you're installing Windows 8 afresh in your home, it's possible to join an active wireless network before you even get to the desktop. As one of the steps during the initial setup procedure, you'll be given a list of the detected networks; choose one and you'll be asked to enter your security password. Do so and when you get into Windows 8 proper, you should have internet access straight away.

(2) ACCESS THE CHARM To connect to a wireless network if you're already in Windows 8, launch the Settings charm by hovering the mouse over the bottom-right corner of the screen until the charms menu appears from the right, then choose the cog symbol to access Settings. On a tablet, swipe a finger inwards from the right-hand bezel and the charms will appear, then tap the Settings cog just as you would with a mouse. You'll see the Settings charm swing open from the right-hand side, ready to use – and this will work whether you're in the traditional desktop or the new Windows 8 home screen.

(3) SETTINGS The Settings charm has several options at the top, but it's the bottom we're most interested in. Among the grid of six symbols – usually in the first spot on the left – you'll see a

Network symbol, which looks like a monitor with a cable at its side (if you're on a wired connection) or a radio symbol (if you're on wireless). Click it and you'll get to a similar menu as in Step 1. Provided Flight mode (which kills all communications) is disabled, any available networks will appear in a list, each with a series of bars to indicate signal strength. Find your network here – check the make of your router or its manual if you don't know what name to look for – and click on its name to enter your password. Your system should now connect without problems.

(4) COMPLICATIONS If you're unable to get your wireless network up and running at the first attempt, there are a few things to try. First, if there's a physical Wi-Fi switch around the base of your laptop, make sure it's set to On, since this can override Windows settings that may otherwise make you think all is well. Make sure your router is plugged in and connected to the net – try switching it off and on again if the connection isn't working. Finally, if all else appears to be operating correctly, locate the Change PC Settings option at the bottom of the Charms menu. Choose the Wireless menu, and run through the settings, making sure you're not in Flight mode, and that your Wi-Fi is set to On in Windows. If everything looks okay, try the above steps again.

HOW LONG?
If your PC and the router are both working normally, it's simple to get them talking.

HOW HARD?
A few clicks and it's done. You shouldn't need to mess with passwords again unless you buy a new router.

IF YOU HAVE MULTIPLE PCs AND LAPTOPS IN YOUR HOME, IT'S USEFUL TO BE
ABLE TO SHARE FILES. THAT'S WHERE A HOMEGROUP COMES IN HANDY

Introducing HomeGroup

HomeGroup is an existing feature that makes a welcome
return in Windows 8. Put simply, it's an easy way to share
files across multiple PCs and laptops in your home. As long
as all of your systems are connected to the same wireless
router, they can be set up to share the files that you want to
share across all of them. Plus, if one system is connected to
a printer, all of the other systems can access the device too.

GROUP THERAPY You can set up a HomeGroup with a few
clicks from any computer in your home running Windows
7 or 8. Once it's created, other PCs running Windows 7 or 8
and connected to the same network can join by entering a
password. You can set this yourself, or you can have a secure
code automatically generated by Windows. The beauty is at
no point do you need to know the name or network address
of any of the other computers.

Once your HomeGroup is up and running, you'll
see it appear in the Windows Explorer navigation pane, with
a list of all the other computers in your HomeGroup that
are online. Simply click into one and you'll be able to access
the Libraries on your other PC as if they were on the one
in front of you. You can even incorporate files from your
HomeGroup into your libraries.

SECURITY Be careful about which libraries you choose to
share across your HomeGroup. Documents is disabled by
default, so you can let your family listen to your music
collection without them having access to your financial
records, for example. You can also manually mark files and
folders as private to prevent anyone else accessing them.
As an extra level of security, all folders are set to read-only
at first; you can give write access to specific folders if you
wish, as we show in the walkthrough opposite. Be warned,
any changes you make apply to everybody – you can't give a
single PC or user access to a file.

GO OFFLINE The bane of any file-sharing arrangement is
finding that a PC containing files you want to access is
offline: even Windows 8 can't talk to a PC that's switched
off. There is a workaround, though. When that PC is on, you
can set its files or folders to be available "offline". You'll find
that you can then access them when the PC is off. To do this,
Windows makes a hidden copy of the file on your own PC –
if your system can't connect to the source PC, it shows you
this copy instead. If the other user changes the file, you'll
only see that update the next time you're both online for the
files to synchronise.

FAQ

Q: Will I be able
to access my
HomeGroup when I'm
away from home?

A: HomeGroup only
works within your
home network, not
over the internet. For
a laptop that regularly
returns home, you could
use offline files; for
computers that
are permanently
on separate networks,
your best option
is to use Windows
SkyDrive instead.
.

Q: Is there a
disadvantage to making
files available offline?

A: It consumes some
space on your hard
disk, so if you're talking
about a large amount of
files it could leave you
short of free space.

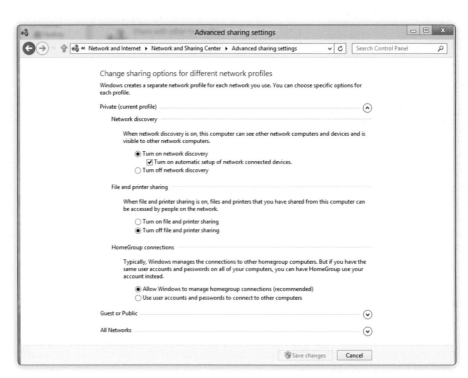

The "Advanced
sharing settings"
screen enables you
to fine-tune which
devices, folders
and files are made
accessible to your
HomeGroup.

HOW TO...
SET UP A HOMEGROUP

 HEAD HOME As we've explained on the previous page, HomeGroup makes the painfully difficult task of sharing files and folders with multiple PCs and laptops over a home network much more bearable. Plus, it takes only a few simple steps to set up.

First, ensure all of your PCs and laptops are connected to the same wireless (or wired) network. You can check by opening the Settings charm and seeing which network is selected.

 GROUP PRESSURE On a new PC or laptop, open the charm, select your home network from the list, and enter the password when asked. When you first connect to a network, you'll be offered the chance to set up a HomeGroup. Using the drop-down boxes in this window, you can specify exactly which types of files and folders you want shared by default here, and whether or not to also stream music and video to all the other PCs in your HomeGroup.

INVITE ONLY After a short pause, a window will appear in which a HomeGroup password will fade into view. You'll notice the password is long and random, which may not be convenient but is certainly secure. You need this password for the next step, so either take a moment to write it down on a Post-it note – or

better still, copy and paste it into a new text document. To make the next bit easier you might want to save that document onto a USB stick, email it to yourself, or move it into cloud storage – you'll need it on the next PC.

 TIME SHARE Once your HomeGroup has been set up on one system, you can join it from any other Windows 7 or Windows 8 computer on the same network simply by clicking the HomeGroup entry that will now be visible in the left-hand pane of any Windows Explorer window.

When the Join HomeGroup box opens, either type in or copy and paste the password from the previous step, select which documents you want to share on this PC, and that's it – your files are shared. You can leave the group at any time from the HomeGroup settings window. You can now also share devices plugged into your main PC, such as an external hard disk or printer, for instance – handy if you need to print something from your laptop.

By default, a HomeGroup will share everything on your system under the banner of Music, Pictures or Video – although that will depend on the options you chose during setup or when joining. If that sounds scary, there is a way to keep a specific file or folder private from everyone else: just go to the top menu bar and click "Share with", then select "Nobody".

HOW LONG?
The great thing about HomeGroup is that you can set it up in seconds.

HOW HARD?
This has been deliberately kept simple – the most difficult step is entering the password.

6

Internet & networking

 THIS IS THE FIRST VERSION OF WINDOWS DESIGNED TO WORK ON 3G-ENABLED TABLETS. WE SHOW YOU HOW TO ACCESS THE INTERNET ON THE MOVE WITH 3G

Using 3G on tablets

Your exciting new Windows 8 tablet has Wi-Fi, and so can connect to the same wireless networks as your PC and laptop when you're at home or in the office. But where tablets really come into their own, in terms of accessing the web, is when you add 3G support to the equation.

Some laptop users may already be familiar with accessing the internet via 3G thanks to a plug-in USB dongle, but with built-in SIM cards the new wave of 3G-enabled Windows 8 tablets operate more like a smartphone than a laptop by connecting directly to 3G phone masts.

Now, it's important to note that not all Windows 8 tablets can do this. If internet on the move is important to you, be sure to choose a tablet that specifically states it has both Wi-Fi and 3G. As more devices are released we may even see some available on contract, as you'd buy a 3G mobile phone, but for now they'll more likely come with a SIM card slot that you can use to get online – the SIM card itself is your responsibility to provide.

USING A DONGLE If you don't have a tablet with 3G support, you can still access the internet on the move like you would on a laptop, by buying a 3G dongle, although it's a fairly unwieldy process. Just go to any mobile phone shop and ask for a dongle, choose a payment plan, then plug the dongle

into the USB port on your tablet. Windows 8 should already have the drivers for most 3G hardware, so you shouldn't have to install anything manually. In fact, it's likely that your biggest worry will be making sure not to snap the dongle off as you carry the tablet around.

Another alternative is to "tether" the tablet to your smartphone. This effectively turns your phone into a Wi-Fi hotspot, with the tablet using your phone's existing 3G connection.

The method for getting online is much the same as for Wi-Fi networks (see p94). Just open the Settings charm and tap the Network icon, and you'll see switches for both Wi-Fi and 3G. Make sure the 3G switch is set to On, and you'll see available 3G networks in a list along with available Wi-Fi networks. You can have your system remember multiple networks, such as the home Wi-Fi and your mobile dongle, and it will always prioritise Wi-Fi over 3G to keep the cost down wherever possible. There's also an Airplane mode for those times when you want to disable all connectivity but still use the tablet's other functions.

PAYING FOR DATA Whether you choose a dongle, a built-in SIM card or tethering, how you pay for downloaded data is a vital consideration. Any mobile phone shop will be able to put you on either a monthly or pay-as-you-go contract. That's

Tip

Be sure to set up Wi-Fi networks on your tablet for all of your regular locations: your home, friends and relatives' homes, the office, even your regular commute if it has free Wi-Fi. That way, whenever you go within range of one of these saved networks, your tablet will automatically connect and use Wi-Fi instead of eating into your valuable 3G data allowance. When you disconnect from the network again, you'll revert to 3G.

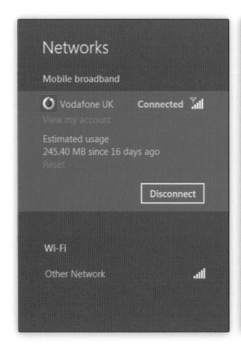

Invest in a 3G Windows 8 tablet and aside from the standard set of wireless network settings, you'll also see a Mobile broadband option listing your 3G account and the amount of data you've consumed recently.

PC settings

Personalize
Pick your colors and pictures.

Users
Change your account or add new ones.

Wireless
Turn wireless and airplane mode on or off.

Notifications
Choose if apps notify you when something's happening.

Privacy
Control how apps use your personal info.

General
Change time zone, keyboard, or language; or reset your PC.

Search
Pick the apps you want to search, or delete your history.

Share
Pick the apps you use to share stuff, or delete your history.

Wireless

Airplane mode
Off

Wireless devices

Mobile broadband
On

Wi-Fi
Off

Bluetooth
On

Mobile broadband hardware

AT&T

Turn on Airplane mode in the Wireless section of the PC settings screen to use your tablet with its Wi-Fi and 3G connectivity disabled.

HOW LONG?
Getting a 3G data contract is the only time-consuming part.

HOW HARD?
If everything is set up at your ISP it should just be a case of turning it on.

Data-heavy video-streaming services such as BBC iPlayer should be set to work only on Wi-Fi internet connections – not over 3G.

the important difference between 3G and Wi-Fi: as with any mobile phone, accessing the internet over 3G sees your data use tallied up, so choose your 3G package based on your data requirements. A wide variety of packages are available, and with a little discipline you can take advantage of Wi-Fi networks cleverly to minimise your 3G data use (see Tip, left).

Pay close attention to the data download limits of each contract, as some seemingly attractive offers come with a small amount of included data – and if you go over your limit you'll start paying considerably more for every megabyte.

Thankfully, Windows 8 includes some useful tools to monitor usage. First, the Networks option expands to show recent estimated data consumption, and has a setting to enable or disable roaming for when you go abroad.

One highly useful option is the ability to limit unnecessary downloads. Open the Settings charm and click Change PC settings, then go to the Devices section. There, below a list of devices connected to your system, is the option to "Download over metered connections". Making sure this is disabled prevents system and app updates from downloading unless you're connected to Wi-Fi. Some updates can be huge, and you don't want the shock of a huge bill for an update you possibly didn't even know had been downloaded.

Finally, below the network name in the Networks Charm you'll see a "View my account" link. Click that and, provided your network supports it, you'll see details of your data plan, your usage and any messages from the provider.

CHECKING YOUR APPS To check which apps are chomping through your 3G data allowance the fastest, use the Windows 8 Task Manager. It now includes details of how much data each Modern UI app has consumed since it was first installed – split into Network and Metered Network use. If you spot a particular data hog, be sure to kill it before leaving your home or office Wi-Fi bubble.

IN THIS CHAPTER

102 Files and folders: the basics:
Navigate your files and folders, and find out what's new in Windows 8's file system.

104 Mastering libraries
Discover how Windows 8 organises your most important documents, photos and files into libraries of related content.

106 Microsoft SkyDrive
Discover Microsoft's integrated cloud storage service and find out how to set up your own account.

7

Handling files and folders

HANDLING FILES

Little has changed when it comes to the file system that underpins Windows 8, so if you have experience of previous versions of Microsoft's operating system, you'll find navigating your files and folders will be almost second nature. That's not to say Microsoft has rested on its laurels in Windows 8, however. We've examined the changes that have been made to the

AND FOLDERS

file-handling system, including new options that make copying and pasting files easier than ever, and there's more information about libraries – the clever system that collates files from across your computer into single folders. There's also more information about Microsoft's SkyDrive, the cloud storage application that's built into Windows 8.

THE NEW INTERFACE LOOKS SNAZZY – BUT, UNDERNEATH, WINDOWS 8 IS BUILT ON A TRIED-AND-TRUSTED CORE THAT MAKES FILE AND FOLDER ACCESS EASY

Files and folders: the basics

The file system is one of the most important parts of an operating system: it underpins everything in an OS such as Windows, governing what files and folders go where, how they interact with applications, and how they can be accessed by the user.

The name of the file system used in Windows is NTFS, which has been the dominant file system since it was first introduced in Windows NT 3.1 way back in 1993. Its inclusion in Windows 8 means that there are no fundamental changes to the way in which most users will interact with files and folders in Microsoft's latest OS.

NEW FOR WINDOWS 8 Many of the most obvious changes when it comes to files and folders are in the copy, paste and delete dialogs. Microsoft has worked hard to add additional features to these parts of the OS, citing third-party applications such as TeraCopy and FastCopy for inspiration.

Copying and pasting still work in the same way: select files you want to move and either right-click to select the relevant option or use the familiar keyboard shortcuts: Ctrl-C to copy, Ctrl-X to cut and Ctrl-V to paste.

Microsoft now incorporates more than one copying or pasting job into its dialog boxes, so multiple operations are now contained within a single box – a much easier solution than making the user hunt through a multitude of dialog boxes. Windows 8 will let you pause, resume and stop jobs as they're in progress, and you can even pause and resume jobs after you've put a PC into its sleep or hibernation modes.

Clicking the names of the folders in question will open them – a new addition to Windows 8 – and a key change makes it much easier to monitor your file transfers, with real-time throughput graphs included in every file operation. These comprehensive diagrams serve up three types of information, with transfer speed, transfer speed trends and the amount of data left presented in one graph.

The other change here comes when Windows 8 discovers duplicate files. Instead of a dry pop-up box that asks whether you'd like to copy, replace or skip the file with no additional information provided, Windows now provides the filenames, sizes, formats and even thumbnail pictures to help you decide if they're truly duplicates. Windows will stuff every potential duplicate into one dialog box, so it's possible to deal with them in batches. It's a much better system than we're used to, especially when it comes to dealing with large numbers of files.

Tip

◢ Many of Windows 8's system files and folders are stored in hidden directories, but if you're doing some advanced tweaking it pays to have them out in the open. Head to the Folder Options dialog, then to the View tab, and select the "Show hidden files, folders and drives" radio button. This will ensure plenty of important files are visible when you're trying to improve your OS, fix a bug, or even free up space by deleting temporary files.

Windows 8 now makes it much easier to deal with duplicate files when you're copying folders from one disk drive to another, clearly marking when the files being transferred are already in the destination folder.

The file-transfer dialog box provides a graph showing the transfer rate and progress of the files being copied. Transfers can be paused midway through if they're harming the performance of your PC.

All of the major file-handling features are now located in the ribbon interface at the top of Windows Explorer windows. However, you can still use the familiar keyboard shortcuts of yesteryear for commands such as copy and paste.

HOW LONG?
If you've used Windows before, then much of Windows 8's file and folder options will be second nature.

HOW HARD?
Windows makes it easy to access files and folders through Explorer and libraries, and new features help too.

ACCESSING FILES AND FOLDERS The lack of major changes to the Windows file system means that anyone familiar with Windows 7 should be able to navigate their files and folders with ease. The Documents, Pictures and Music folders are largely the same, for example, and those used to the libraries introduced in Windows 7 will be able to get to grips with them here. We've also delved into the intricacies and new features of libraries on p104.

The new Windows 8 interface means there's another layer between users and their files and folders, at least initially, but it's easy enough to add shortcuts to your most popular folders to the Windows 8 Start screen: simply right-click on the folder and select "Pin to Start".

It's not the only option that makes getting to your files and folders simpler. Jump Lists make a welcome return, and can be used to access recent and frequently accessed files in applications you've pinned to the Windows desktop taskbar. Pin Microsoft Word to the taskbar, for instance, and right-clicking on its icon opens up a list of recently accessed files. Up to 60 can be stored in each Jump List, and favourite documents can be pinned to the list so they're never knocked off the bottom by more recent documents.

The Control Panel plays host to a variety of file and folder options, most of which have remained unchanged from Windows 7. Basic options allow for the customisation of folder opening actions, and you're able to choose which folders are listed in the navigation pane of Explorer windows.

The View tab of the Folder Options menu provides more complex options for tweaking the look and feel of files and folders within Windows, including settings for showing hidden files and folders.

The Search tab has options for tweaking results when searching for files and folders from the Windows 8 Start screen. Microsoft has made minor changes to the file and folder search functionality since Windows 7; it's still possible to find partial matches and turn off the search index, but the option to deactivate subfolder inclusion has disappeared, as has the natural language search.

Windows 8 still allows you to include system directories and compressed files in your searches, and it's now possible to prevent the operating system from searching through the contents of files – an option included to save time, especially on slower machines.

COLLECT DOCUMENTS, PICTURES, MUSIC AND MOVIES INTO ONE FOLDER FROM ACROSS YOUR PC OR YOUR ENTIRE NETWORK BY USING LIBRARIES

Mastering libraries

Head beyond the Windows 8 interface and you'll find a feature that will be familiar to anyone who's spent time with Windows 7: the libraries that are used to collate a wide variety of files used in the operating system.

At first glance, and like many of the features on Windows 8's desktop, little has changed. Four libraries are used to store documents, pictures, videos and music files, with files grouped together from different sources (such as your PC's hard disk and external disk drives) and folders.

LIBRARIES: THE BASICS Delve into the four libraries in Windows 8 and you'll find several new features and a handful of changes in a couple of key areas. The first, titled "Manage library", allows for easier access to the library customisation options that were included in Windows 7.

It's possible to add additional folders to each library, and each folder can be chosen as the default save location for new files. Folders can also be removed, and each library can be optimised for particular types of file, with options available for general folders, documents, music, pictures and videos.

Libraries in Windows 8 also benefit from the ribbon interface that was introduced in Microsoft Office

2007. This makes it easier to see the full range of options available from libraries, from deleting and renaming files to altering the properties of each library in turn.

The Pictures, Music and Movies libraries all included specific tools in their ribbon menus. The Pictures option includes the ability to rotate an image, set a picture as a desktop background and start a slideshow, as well as the ability to send images to external devices.

The Music and Videos libraries share the same additional options as the Pictures library. It's possible to play music and video files directly from the ribbon; simply hit the button and Windows Media Player will open automatically. You can also send files to other devices and play them directly, with compatibility included for smartphones and media players attached to the PC.

If opening an Explorer window is too much like hard work, it's possible to pin the Library folder, or individual libraries, to your Windows 8 Start screen. To do this, just right-click on the library and choose "Pin to Start".

If anything should go wrong with your libraries when you're renaming or creating bespoke libraries of your own (see walkthrough, left), right-click on the Libraries label in the left-hand panel, and select Restore Default Libraries.

Tip

If you're trying to share music or movies from a Windows 8 library to an external device, make sure you have the right driver installed. Android smartphones, for instance, won't interact with a PC until the correct driver or software package has been installed. If you're playing a file locally, search for Default Programs and choose which application you'd like to use when playing back. Windows 8 uses Windows Media Player out of the box, but there's nothing stopping you from picking your own application.

The ribbon interface added to Windows Explorer makes it easier to find options for handling files in libraries, offering options tailored to the type of file, such as playback buttons for music and video files.

HOW TO...
CUSTOMISE YOUR LIBRARIES

① TWEAK THE DEFAULT LIBRARIES Like Windows 7, Windows 8 provides four default libraries: one each for Documents, Music, Pictures and Videos. They're set up to work pretty much out of the box, but libraries are all about versatility, so it's worth customising these four folders to work precisely as you'd prefer.

To customise your existing libraries, simply right-click on a library and select Properties. The first window is used to determine which folders contribute to each library. Select a folder and click the Remove button if you'd like its files to stop appearing in each library. If you'd like to add a folder, click Include a Folder and navigate to its location. It doesn't have to be a local folder, either: libraries can collate files from other computers on your home network and external disks, too.

The small tick beside a folder indicates which folder is used to store new files that are saved to a library. If you'd like to change this, select the folder you'd like to use and click the Set Save Location button.

② CREATE YOUR OWN LIBRARIES If none of the four options suits your needs, it's easy to create your own. You might, for example, choose to create separate libraries for work and personal documents. Navigate to the main library window or simply right-click on the Libraries link in the navigation pane, head to the New menu and select Library. The new library appears instantly, and its name is selected by default – just type in a new name and hit Enter.

New for Windows 8 is the ability to change the icon used. Simply right-click on the library, select Properties, and hit the "Change library icon" button at the bottom. There are a selection of stock Windows icons to pick from, or you can browse your PC for custom icons.

③ OPTIMISE LIBRARIES The four default libraries include bespoke options pertinent to the types of files stored in each location, but those aren't activated on libraries that you've created. To activate the options, right-click on the library, head to the Properties menu, and select the type of file (such as documents) from the Optimise This Library For... drop-down menu. Depending on the option chosen, your new library will offer the range of options we've described opposite.

④ SHARE YOUR LIBRARIES Any library can be connected to networked folders. To set this up, head to the Properties menu, choose Include a Folder and navigate to your NAS drive or cloud storage folder in order to incorporate its documents.

This isn't the only sharing option that's available, either. Right-click on a library or on the files and folders within a library, and head to the "Share With" option. You'll be given the option to grant access to other user accounts on your PC or in your HomeGroup, and it's also possible to enter email addresses into the box that appears. This allows you to give read and write permission to those outside of your immediate network.

HOW LONG?
If you've used Windows 7 libraries, you'll have no problems getting to grips with Windows 8.

HOW HARD?
It's easy to get started with libraries, but incorporating network locations and sharing libraries is trickier.

1

2

3

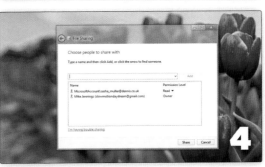

4

SKYDRIVE IS MICROSOFT'S BUILT-IN CLOUD STORAGE SERVICE. HERE WE'LL SHOW YOU HOW TO MAKE THE MOST OF THIS USEFUL FEATURE

Microsoft SkyDrive

The increasing availability of high-speed internet has seen a boom in cloud-based file services, with products such as Dropbox and SugarSync gaining massive popularity with those who want to share and back up files with as little fuss as possible. Microsoft's SkyDrive has been around since 2007, but its inclusion in Windows 8 is the first time it's been fully integrated into the operating system.

If you've signed into Windows 8 using a Microsoft account, you'll find you can access your SkyDrive folders right away, either from the app on the new Start menu or via the link in Windows Explorer.

THE BASICS SkyDrive is a cloud storage service that allows users to upload files to Microsoft's servers. It's then possible to log in to https://skydrive.live.com and browse, download, open and even edit these files from any internet-enabled PC.

SkyDrive can be installed on multiple machines and, as long as they have an internet connection, files will be synchronised between PCs, laptops and mobile devices: upload a file using SkyDrive on one device, and it will be accessible on the rest.

Everyone who signs up for SkyDrive receives 7GB of free storage – that compares well with the 2GB included with Dropbox – and it's also possible to pay for additional space: a £6 annual fee will grant you 20GB of additional space; £16 per year gives access to 50GB of room; and if you're willing to pay £32 every year, you can add 100GB to your SkyDrive account. Individual files can be up to 300MB in size if they're uploaded using the web client, but files of up to 2GB in size are supported if uploaded using the full desktop application.

SkyDrive applications are available for Windows Vista, 7 and OS X Lion or any later versions, and also for Windows Phone and Apple iOS.

SKYDRIVE FEATURES Documents stored in SkyDrive can be accessed, created, edited and shared from within the app's web browser interface using Microsoft Office Web Apps, and there's even support for multiple users to co-author Excel and OneNote documents. Integration with Microsoft Office is impressive, too: edits can be made by different users to the same document simultaneously when it's accessed through SkyDrive.

Office documents can also be embedded into web pages, so those visiting pages with embedded PowerPoint files can view your presentation, for instance. SkyDrive supports several file formats, and its built-in search can hunt through documents created using Office formats.

Documents and photos can be directly uploaded to SkyDrive from within the Hotmail and Outlook.com email services, and integration with Facebook, Twitter and LinkedIn enables users to share files with contacts on their respective networks.

Photos with geolocation data are displayed alongside a map of where they were taken, uploaded pictures can be viewed as a slideshow, and entire folders can be compressed and downloaded as Zip files, up to a limit of either 4GB or 65,000 files per Zip file.

Tip

SkyDrive folders can be added to Windows 8 libraries, so the files stored here can be viewed alongside documents and files collated from all over the rest of your PC. It's easy enough to do: open a Windows Explorer window on the desktop and right-click the SkyDrive entry. The first option in the context menu is "Include in library" – simply enter this menu and choose which library you'd like to use.

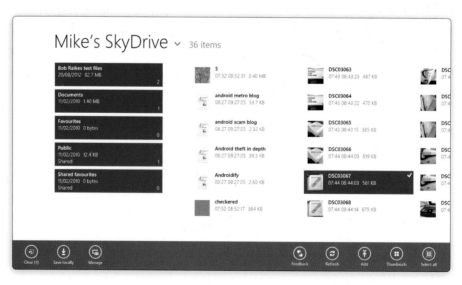

Photos can be shared across multiple devices with SkyDrive.

HOW TO...
SET UP YOUR SKYDRIVE

 REGISTER FOR SKYDRIVE It's easy to get started with SkyDrive. If you log into Windows 8 using a Windows Live account, then you've already activated your SkyDrive account – just click on the tile on the Windows 8 Start screen to access it. If you need to create a new account for SkyDrive, head to https:// skydrive.live.com. Signing up requires your name, date of birth, and other standard details. Be sure to choose a username you'll remember and, just as importantly, a password that's as secure as possible.

 UPLOAD FILES Click the SkyDrive tile on the Start screen, make sure you're logged in and you'll be taken to the main interface. At the bottom of the window is an icon called Upload – click it, and you'll be able to add all manner of files to your SkyDrive. The default window lists everything in your Documents folder: simply click what you'd like to upload, and the files will be highlighted.

Click the Files title at the top of the window and you can change which folder you use to upload; it's possible to choose from your Pictures, Videos and Download folders, the desktop, and even other PCs or NAS drives on your home network. SkyDrive can take pictures using any attached webcam and upload them, too. Once you've chosen your files, click Add to SkyDrive and they will be uploaded. A progress indicator will appear in the top right-hand corner of the main SkyDrive window. Click on it to see status bars for every file you're uploading. One word of warning: it's not possible to upload entire folders from SkyDrive's Windows 8 app.

 USE SKYDRIVE ON THE DESKTOP As well as being integrated into the Windows 8 interface, SkyDrive is now available on the desktop. It appears in the Favorites section of Explorer windows, and functions in the same way as other folders found in this area. Clicking the SkyDrive icon brings up its folders in the right-hand pane of the Explorer window. These can be navigated in the same way as any other Windows folder, and it's also possible to drag and drop entire folders into SkyDrive folders – something that you can't do in the Modern app.

MANAGE YOUR FILES SkyDrive includes several file-management options. The app included with Windows 8 serves up several options from the bottom of the screen if you right-click on a file or folder. Right-click on a file, for example, and you can save the file locally, delete it or open it in relevant applications; it will suggest the default application for different types of file, but click "More options" to choose a different application.

Additional options are available if you're interacting with SkyDrive from Windows Explorer. Here, the traditional range of options can be used: left-click to open a file or folder, and right-click to open the context menu and access options for editing, sharing and opening the document.

HOW LONG?
It takes a little while to establish the ideal file regime in your personal SkyDrive, but once that's done, it's an efficient way of accessing your files on multiple devices.

HOW HARD?
SkyDrive isn't packed with options, and it's easy to set up and get sharing.

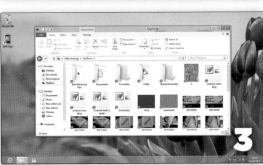

IN THIS CHAPTER

110 Restore, refresh and reinstall

If something goes wrong, you can easily restore Windows 8 to a working state.

112 Backing up your data

Windows 8's File History feature makes it effortless to keep your precious files safe.

114 Windows Update

Ensure your system is stable and secure by installing the latest updates from Microsoft.

116 Family Safety

The internet can be a dangerous place, but Windows 8's built-in tools can keep your kids safe.

118 Action Center

Get proactive warnings when there's a potential problem with your system or settings.

120 Windows Defender

Windows' built-in scanner can stop viruses and other online nasties in their tracks.

122 Windows Firewall

Don't want strangers connecting to your PC? The Firewall keeps them firmly locked out.

124 User Account Control

A simple security feature that keeps you in control of what happens on your system.

126 Third-party security software

There's plenty of security software out there; we compare some of the biggest names.

8
Security

SECURITY

Windows 8 contains a wealth of features for ensuring things run smoothly and stably. In this chapter we'll look at ways to restore your PC when things go wrong, and how to back up your valuable files using the new File History feature. We'll also look at using Family Safety to ensure your children stay safe online; and we introduce the Action Center, which can give you

an early warning if something isn't right. We'll show you how Windows Defender and the Windows Firewall keep you safe from viruses and cyber-attacks, and how to configure them to work the way you want. We also explain how Windows 8's User Account Control system prevents your settings being changed, and look at the best third-party security software that's out there.

ROLLING BACK WINDOWS TO AN EARLIER STATE MAY SOUND LIKE A DRASTIC MEASURE, BUT WITH WINDOWS 8 IT'S A SAFE AND EASY OPTION

Restore, refresh and reinstall

Even with a modern operating system such as Windows 8, things can go wrong. It's possible that a badly written program might mess up your settings, for example, or that a virus could interfere with the way your computer works. In a scenario such as this, your first step is obvious: try removing the suspect program, and install security software to detect and remove any malware (something we'll discuss in more depth later in this chapter).

If these measures don't work, however, it's time to consider reverting your PC to an earlier, working state. The easiest way to do this is using Windows' System Restore feature – a tool you might already be familiar with, as it's been present in all versions of Windows since XP. Simply put, it runs in the background and automatically notes changes to system files and settings. If need be, Windows can then be reverted to the state it was in at a previous point in time simply by undoing these changes.

To access System Restore, go to the Windows 8 Control Panel or open a Settings search from the Start screen and search for an item called "Recovery". Click Open System Restore on the pane that appears and you'll see a list of recent changes that were made to your system: click "Show more restore points" to see points from more than a few days ago. Choose one and click "Next" and

your PC will be reverted to that state. Note, however, that your personal documents won't be touched.

To give System Restore the best chance of remedying problems, it's a good idea to let it keep a long history of changes made to your system while Windows is running smoothly. Happily, this is Windows 8's default setup. If you're short on hard disk storage you might be tempted to save space by deleting old System Restore points or disabling the feature altogether (both options are available through the Control Panel). However, we'd urge you to resist this temptation.

REFRESHING THE PC If System Restore doesn't help, the next step to consider is refreshing your PC. Refresh is a new feature in Windows 8 that automatically reinstalls the operating system from scratch to ensure that everything is in pristine condition. This isn't as drastic a step as it may sound: Windows 8 is smart enough to preserve your documents and personal settings, as well as some important configuration features such as network, encryption and mobile broadband settings. Refreshing doesn't have to be a major upheaval.

Refresh comes with a few caveats. The first is that any desktop applications installed on your PC will be wiped

PC settings

Personalize

Users

Notifications

Search

Spelling

Autocorrect misspelled words
On

Highlight misspelled words
On

Language

Add or change input methods, keyboard layouts, and languages.
Language preferences

Refresh your PC

Here's what will happen:
- Your files and personalization settings won't change.
- Your PC settings will be changed back to their defaults.
- Apps from Windows Store will be kept.
- Apps you installed from discs or websites will be removed.
- A list of removed apps will be saved on your desktop.

Next   Cancel

HomeGroup

Windows Update

If you want to recycle your PC or start over completely, you can reset it to its factory settings.
Get started

Advanced startup

Start up from a device or disc (such as a USB drive or DVD), change Windows startup settings, or restore Windows from a system image. This will restart your PC.
Restart now

Refreshing your PC reinstalls Windows 8, but leaves all your documents untouched.

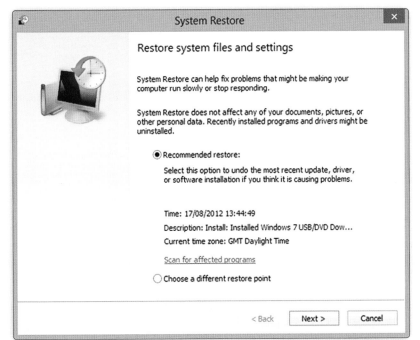

System Restore works in the same way as it did in previous versions of Windows, taking your PC back to a working state.

HOW LONG?
On a typical PC the process takes around 15 minutes.

HOW HARD?
All that's needed is a few mouse clicks to get the process going.

as part of the process, and you'll need to reinstall them. So before refreshing your PC, check that you have all the installation discs, licence keys and so forth that you'll need to restore your PC to a fully usable condition. Modern apps aren't erased, because there's no need: they don't "hook into" your system in the way that desktop software does, so there's nothing to be gained by removing them.

Our second warning about Refresh is that, although it tries to leave your data untouched, it may not necessarily be able to identify every data file on your system, especially if your files are in unusual places and have unusual filenames. Before running Refresh it's a good idea to make sure everything important to you is located in a personal location (such as the Documents library or the desktop). For complete peace of mind, we recommend ensuring you have a complete backup of your system (see overleaf for our guide to backups).

CLEAN INSTALL What if your system is clogged up with too many personal files and you decide you simply want to wipe the PC and start again? In previous editions of Windows, this was a big deal: to achieve it you'd commonly have to boot from a special DVD provided by your PC manufacturer, or from a specially prepared partition on your hard disk, and wait upwards of an hour as Windows was painstakingly reinstalled along with all necessary drivers and third-party add-ons.

In Windows 8, life is much easier. In Settings, you'll find a new option called "Remove everything and reinstall Windows". This does precisely what it says: follow the process and in as little as 10 minutes – depending on the speed of your PC and the erasure method you choose – Windows will be reinstalled in a completely pristine state.

All your desktop applications and Metro apps will be gone, along with all your personal data and settings.

Reinstall is a useful feature if you've made a mess of Windows and want to start again, or if you need to pass your computer on to someone else. If this is your plan, it's worth choosing the "thorough" erasure method rather than the "quick" one. Although the thorough method takes longer to execute, it overwrites all your data files to ensure that the data they contained is physically erased from the disk, and that they can't be recovered by anybody. If you pick the quick erasure method, it's possible that someone armed with the right software could come along and salvage your old files.

Windows 8 includes a number of troubleshooting options to help you out if things go wrong with the operating system.

IT'S ALWAYS A GOOD IDEA TO KEEP BACKUPS OF YOUR PERSONAL FILES – AND WINDOWS 8 MAKES IT EASIER THAN EVER

Backing up your data

System Restore and Refresh can save the day if Windows runs into problems. But what if you hit a hardware problem? Hard disks fail, CDs get scratched and USB drives are mislaid. And if you lose a spreadsheet or email archive, you can't simply reinstall it: such personal data is irreplaceable.

But all isn't lost if you plan ahead and keep backups. There are plenty of backup systems on offer, from basic freeware packages to advanced systems that can create backup images of your entire hard disk and monitor a whole network. Windows 8 includes a fully functional backup client that can regularly save your files to a specified destination and even create a backup image of your system. It's hidden away in the Settings, though, under the rather unhelpful name "Windows 7 File Recovery" – indicating that it's provided primarily to allow you to restore backups created in the previous version of Windows.

That's because Windows 8 introduces a much easier and more powerful backup system, called File History. This uses an external hard disk to store backup copies of files as you create, update and delete them. You can browse these versions at the click of a button from Explorer, and preview and restore them whenever you choose.

If you've used a Mac, this idea may sound familiar, as File History is similar to Apple's Time Machine. Opposite you'll find a guide to setting up backups with File History.

CLOUD BACKUP If your main PC is a laptop, it may be inconvenient to keep an external disk plugged in – and if your home is burgled or a fire breaks out, your backup drive could be lost along with your PC. For this reason, some people prefer third-party "cloud" backup services that upload your precious files to a remote server somewhere else in the world. These services use strong encryption to ensure the files can't be read by anyone else.

To use a cloud backup service, you'll need a reliable internet connection; without one, you're unprotected. This could be a showstopper for laptop users who spend a lot of time out on the road.

What's more, it's much slower than using a hard disk. Backing up a 100GB media folder could take weeks of solid uploading, tying up your connection and leaving you only partly protected in the meantime. If disaster does strike then recovering your files can take days. And if you have a capped or metered internet connection, it'll eat up your bandwidth allowance, too.

All the same, for complete peace of mind, online backup adds a degree of security that a local hard disk can't match, and it doesn't have to be expensive: shop around and you can find a service with unlimited storage for around £60 a year. Online backup is also sometimes included in security suites, which we'll come to later in this chapter.

Tip

File History is a Windows 8-only feature, but if you have a mixture of PCs in your house, you can use your File History disk as a shared destination for scheduled backups from other operating systems.

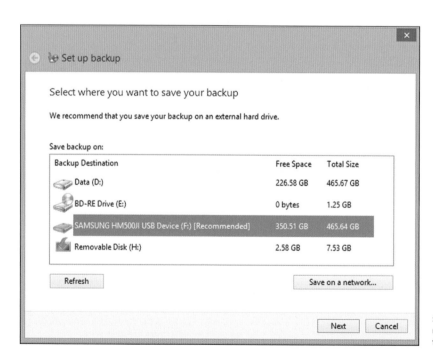

Setting up a decent backup regime is vital to protect your files in case of disaster.

HOW TO...
USE FILE HISTORY

(1) TURN ON FILE HISTORY File History is switched off by default, but when you plug in a USB hard disk a tile appears at the top-right of your screen inviting you to "tap to choose what happens with removable drives". Click on this tile and you'll see the top option is "Configure this drive for backup". You can also search for File History under Settings from the Start screen. Click the "Turn on" button below the disk you want to use and Windows will start backing up the content of your desktop and libraries, plus your contacts, favourite websites and your SkyDrive. If you want other folders to be backed up, you must include them in a library.

(2) CHOOSE A BACKUP LOCATION File History doesn't only work with USB disks. Click "Select drive" on the left and you can choose to back up your files to internal disks and flash drives too. If you want to use a network share or NAS device for your File History backups, choose "Add network location" to open a network browser and select a shared volume.

If you're connected to a HomeGroup (see Chapter 6), once you select a disk you'll be given the option of recommending it to other members of the group running Windows 8; tick this and a pop-up appears on their PC inviting them to use your disk for File History too.

(3) ALTER THE FREQUENCY OF BACKUPS The initial backup can take a few hours if your hard disk is very full: once it's done, changes are automatically backed up every hour. To change the frequency of your backups, click on "Advanced settings" at the left of the File History pane; you can pick a setting from every ten minutes to once a day.

You can also choose how much space should be reserved for the offline cache – this stores copies of backups so they're accessible even if your external hard disk is unplugged or, Heaven forbid, breaks down. You can also enable or disable recommending the drive to other HomeGroup users, and view logs.

(4) RESTORE YOUR FILES With File History running, clicking "Restore personal files" opens a History browser showing previous states of your system. Use the arrows at the bottom to move forwards and backwards in time, and the centre button to restore selected files. Buttons at the bottom right let you view details or thumbnails of files' content; right-click and select Preview to watch videos or play music files; or click a specific file in Windows Explorer, then the History button on the Home tab, to view previous versions. To recover a deleted file, open the History of the containing folder.

HOW LONG?
Plug in an external drive and you can be protected in only 20 minutes.

HOW HARD?
Setting up File History is a matter of a few clicks.

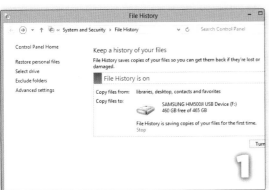

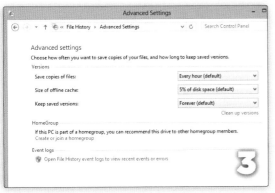

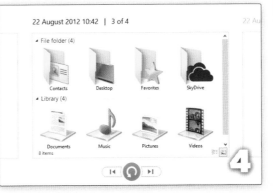

8
Security

INSTALLING REGULAR UPDATES KEEPS YOUR SYSTEM STABLE AND SECURE.
FORTUNATELY, WINDOWS 8 CAN DO ALL THE HARD WORK FOR YOU

Windows Update

Once upon a time, installing an operating system was a one-off job: once it was done, you might run for years with the same system files. These days, computing moves much faster, and it's expected that the operating system installed on your PC will, for the entire duration of its working life, receive regular enhancements via Windows Update.

The Windows Update system in Windows 8 may seem confusing, because it appears in two different places in the operating system. In the Modern-style PC Settings screen, the Windows Update option brings up a one-click Windows Update interface. Desktop users can also access the familiar Windows 7-style interface: to do this, open the Control Panel and click on System and Security | Windows Update. If you just want to install updates, it doesn't matter which you use, but if you want to change any settings you'll need to use the classic interface.

The purpose of Windows Update is simply to ensure the operating system is as smooth and stable as it can be. Windows 8 is a tremendously complex piece of software, and it's expected to work with a vast array of hardware and applications. With the best will in the world, it's almost inevitable that conflicts will arise, causing the system to behave unpredictably or even crash. By pushing out updates to resolve such problems as soon as they're discovered, Microsoft can minimise the disruption and ensure most users have a trouble-free existence.

Updates can also be used to close off security holes. Cybercriminals are constantly seeking ways to compromise your PC with malware or with remote access hacks. Again, by regularly updating the system to patch any security weaknesses as they're found, Microsoft can keep Windows 8 users safe.

As a welcome side-effect, Windows Update can also improve performance by making sure you have the latest versions of the correct software drivers for all your hardware. Alongside the critical fixes, it will also deliver "recommended" updates such as new Help files or upgraded device drivers.

AUTOMATIC INSTALLATION When you first install the operating system, or you start up your new Windows 8 computer for the first time, you may be prompted to configure how Windows updates are delivered. You can also access these configuration options by opening the Start screen and searching Settings for "Turn automatic updating on or off".

You'll see a few options to choose from governing how updates are delivered to your PC: for example, you might wish to be notified when new updates are available, so you can download and install them at your leisure. The default option, however, is to download and install all critical updates automatically.

Tip

Windows Update is suspended when you're on a metered connection, such as a 3G dongle (see Chapter 6), so you don't need to worry about sizeable updates running up horrendous mobile data bills.

You can choose to be notified ahead of updates being installed, if you wish.

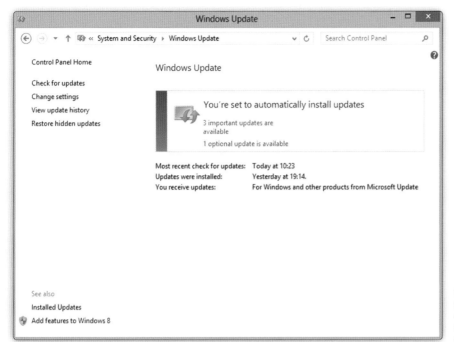

Windows Update keeps you fully informed about what your system needs to stay stable and up to date.

HOW LONG?
Installing periodic updates takes only a minute or two.

HOW HARD?
By default, everything happens automatically.

This setting has long been something of a bone of contention among Windows users, because in order to upgrade fundamental system components it's necessary to shut down Windows completely before restarting it. Previous versions of the operating system used to nag the user to do this whenever an important update was downloaded, and if you didn't do anything the system would eventually reboot itself, potentially causing the user to lose unsaved work.

Happily, Windows 8 calms things down a bit. Now only the most critical security patches require a restart – all other updates will quietly wait until whenever you next choose to reboot. This means you'll normally only be forced to restart your system once a month, when Microsoft releases its regular round of security updates. This takes place on the second Tuesday of each month (colloquially therefore known as "Patch Tuesday") – although if an urgent threat is discovered, Microsoft has on occasion been known to issue the odd off-schedule patch.

Windows 8 is also more relaxed about when a reboot is required. Once a critical update has been downloaded, Windows 8 will notify you for three full days before forcing a reboot, so you should have no problem finding the time to restart the operating system.

There are still situations in which automatic updating is best disabled: if, for example, you're away from home and trying to connect to your PC remotely. In cases such as this, it makes sense to disable automatic updating.

For everyday use, though, we strongly recommend you accept the default setting and allow Windows Update to run automatically. It's much less intrusive than it used to be, and will ensure you always have the best possible protection against system errors and hacker attacks.

UPDATES FOR OTHER APPLICATIONS It's not only Windows that needs regular updates. Viruses have been known to hide in Word documents and PDFs, and vulnerabilities in your browser can provide an easy route for trojans to get on to your system. To be safe, it's best to keep all the programs on your PC up to date. Many applications offer a built-in "Check for updates" option, and third-party update-checkers such as UpdateStar (www.updatestar.com) can help too.

If you install Microsoft Office or other Microsoft applications, you may be given the option to turn Windows Update into a more general Microsoft Update centre. You can find this option by opening the Control Panel and clicking on System and Security | Windows Update, then clicking "Get updates for other Microsoft products".

Note, however, that the latest version of the software, Office 2013, looks after its own updates, keeping each application in step with its equivalent Office 365 component. To see the status of Office 2013 updates, click File | Account | Office Updates.

8
Security

Family Safety

Allowing your kids on the home PC is a crucial part of their education these days – but give an inexperienced user unfettered access and you're asking for trouble. Windows 8 includes a comprehensive set of parental controls to ensure your children don't stray across inappropriate content or inadvertently compromise your security. It also ensures they don't stay up all night chatting or playing games.

Windows 8's individual user accounts make it easy to configure custom settings for your children. All you need to do is create an account for each child, then confirm that you want to apply Family Safety settings to this account. If you want to use Family Safety with an account that already exists, open the Family Safety pane in the Control Panel, click on the relevant account, and select the radio button at the top of the window that opens to apply restrictions.

Family Safety's main role is allowing or blocking certain types of websites and downloads, to help keep your child safe from mature content and malware. This works at the operating system level, so kids can't get around it by switching to a new web browser. But it's versatile: if a child finds that a site they want to access is blocked, you can enable it immediately by entering your password. If you're not around, the child can click a button to email an access request to you, to review and respond to at a later point.

You can restrict which games your children can play, based on ratings issued by the British Board of Film Classification (BBFC) and Pan-European Game Information (PEGI). If you enable Activity Reporting, you can keep an eye on which websites and programs your child is accessing.

THE FAMILY SAFETY WEBSITE In previous versions of Windows, Family Safety was controlled partly from your PC and partly from the Family Safety website. In Windows 8, almost everything can be controlled from within the system. However, if you have more than one child, the website makes it easy to keep track of multiple accounts and PCs. To access the site, click the button "Manage settings on the Family Safety website". This will open your browser (and you'll be asked to provide your password once more).

Once you're in, you'll see a list of all the child accounts attached to your parent account. Here you can monitor and configure settings, and you can also browse a more comprehensive activity report, giving full details of which sites were visited, when, and which applications the user has been running. If you see a blocked site which is in fact appropriate, you can enable it from here. You can also monitor a complete list of requests, to review sites, games and apps your children have requested access to.

Tip

Kids are clever at finding ways around restrictions. Family Safety settings are secured with your account password, so make sure your kids don't find out what this is. If they do, they can log on as you and use the computer without restrictions – and all your work setting up parental controls will be for nothing. Also bear in mind that no filtering system is infallible, and that no automated system is a substitute for vigilant parenting.

Setting up Family Safety to keep your kids – and your PC – safe is a breeze.

HOW TO...
SET UP FAMILY SAFETY

① CHOOSE YOUR LEVEL OF PROTECTION Open the Family Safety User Settings pane. The first option you'll see under Windows settings is the web-filtering module. Click on it to choose a protection level: the most restrictive setting blocks all websites except a shortlist of "child-friendly" sites, or sites approved by you. For older kids, basic filtering opens up most of the web but excludes known pornographic or violent sites, plus pages related to hacking. It's up to you whether you allow access to social networking, web chat and webmail sites. For older children, you can choose to allow access to all websites, but show a warning when a site contains suspected adult content.

② SET TIME LIMITS The second option you'll see under Windows settings is time limits, which enables you to set a maximum amount of time for which each user is permitted to use the PC each day, as well as restrict the specific times at which children can use the PC. If you choose that a user can "only use the PC during the time ranges I allow", you'll see a grid representing the times during which this user account will be accessible. Using the mouse, you can click to permit or block access in half-hour chunks. You could, for example, block off the PC after bedtime and in the morning.

③ SET UP APPLICATION AND GAMES RESTRICTIONS The last two options under Windows settings are Game and Windows Store Restrictions and App Restrictions. These can be used to prevent kids from using certain programs – such as BitTorrent clients commonly used for downloading pirated movies and music, for example – and from running games and Windows 8 apps that are rated above their age group. You can also opt to block any game that doesn't have an official rating, and block or allow specific games. If a child attempts to launch a game or application that you've blocked, they can send you a message requesting permission to run it (or you can type in your password there and then).

④ REPORT ACTIVITY When all is set up to your satisfaction, you can hand the system over to your child with a degree of confidence (see Tip, left). The Activity reporting radio button provides extra peace of mind. With this feature active, at the right of the pane you'll see a link labelled "View activity report": click on this for an overview of the account's most popular websites visited, pages blocked, time spent online and most-used apps and games. If you have several children to watch over, the Family Safety website provides an easier way to monitor and administer several accounts at once.

HOW LONG?
You can set up safety settings for a child in only a few minutes.

HOW HARD?
There are a few separate technical stages to setting up and using Family Safety, but it's all quite straightforward.

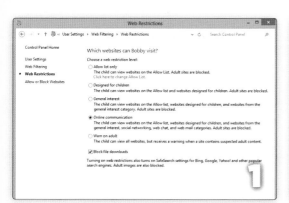

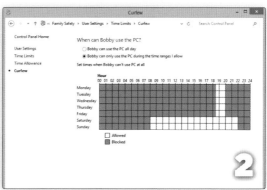

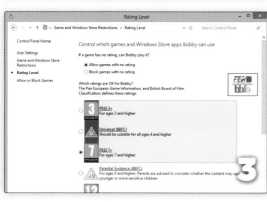

8
Security

Action Center

As we've mentioned, Windows 8 is a tremendously complex system. Although the front-end may be simple, there's a terrific amount going on behind the scenes, and it's governed by hundreds of technical settings. Even for a computer expert, keeping track of all those processes and settings, to make sure your computer is secure and properly configured, is a daunting task.

Happily, Windows 8 anticipates this problem. The Action Center brings all the most important security and maintenance settings into one place, so you can check at a glance that everything is as it ought to be. What's more, when something important is amiss, the Action Center doesn't wait for you to notice: it flags up the problem in a clear, yet unobtrusive, way.

MONITORING SETTINGS The Action Center is found within the desktop Control Panel, under System and Security. If there are any warnings awaiting your attention, you'll see them as soon as you open the pane. A yellow border is used to flag issues that could affect the security or performance of your PC, while a red border is used to draw your attention to urgent problems. In all cases, you'll see a description of the problem, and a button to open the relevant tool or configuration window to address it. Alternatively, you can dismiss the alert by clicking "Turn off messages".

Click the two drop-down icons and you'll see the full range of potential issues monitored by the Action Center. Eighteen areas are covered, divided into Security and Maintenance. These are listed in a somewhat random order, and (slightly frustratingly) if there isn't a problem with an item on the list, no link to the relevant settings is provided, so if you want to tinker you'll have to do a bit of searching. Overall, though, it's a good spread.

SECURITY ACTIONS Under the security heading you'll see the status of all of Windows' most important self-defence mechanisms. This includes your Windows Update settings (see p114) as well as the status of Windows Defender, the Windows Firewall and your User Account Control settings, which we'll address in depth in the coming pages.

It may not be immediately obvious what some other items listed under Security relate to. Windows SmartScreen, for example, is a feature originating in Internet Explorer, which was designed to warn you when you visited a potentially dangerous website. Now in Windows 8 the SmartScreen concept has been expanded to cover all application software. By default, Windows will refuse to install or run unrecognised software without authorisation from an Administrator account (see Chapter 2). If you wish, you can change this to warn you before

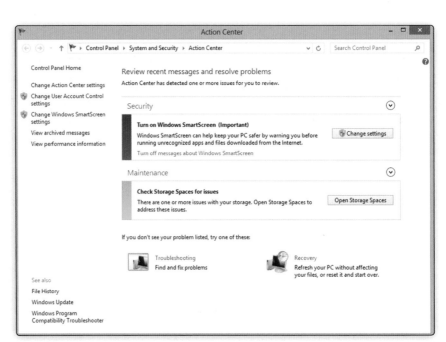

Action Center flags up urgent problems with a red border, while less urgent issues are marked in yellow.

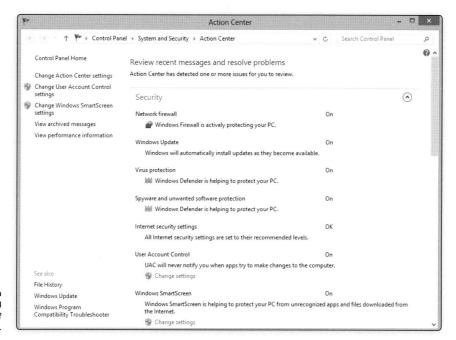

The Security section keeps you up to speed with the status of Windows 8's defences.

HOW LONG?
When a problem is detected, Action Center can resolve it in moments.

HOW HARD?
You don't need to lift a finger: Action Center will pipe up when there is something you need to know about.

running unknown applications, or to allow all software to run. However, if you use one of these less secure settings, Action Center will flag it as a potential issue unless you choose to disable messages about SmartScreen.

Another slightly esoteric Security listing is Network Access Protection. It's highly likely that Windows 8 will report that this feature is "not running" on your PC, yet it won't be flagged as a problem. This is because the feature is normally used only on corporate networks, rather than home computers. Its purpose is to prevent systems not meeting certain security criteria – such as those not running a firewall – from connecting to a network. In a home environment, there's no need to worry about it.

The Security section also includes links to your Window Activation and Microsoft Account settings, so you can check that your copy of Windows has been successfully activated, and review your user and password details.

MAINTENANCE The items monitored under Maintenance focus as much on general system information as on warnings of problems. Here you can see at a glance if you're connected to a HomeGroup, and whether you might be able

to speed up your system by disabling startup applications from the Task Manager. You'll also be notified here if updated hardware drivers or support software is available for something that's plugged into your PC.

There are a few potentially important things to keep an eye on here: if one of your drives isn't working properly, or if something is preventing File History from working, you'll naturally want to know about it.

The good thing about Action Center is that you don't need to keep revisiting it to check that everything is okay. If it thinks a problem might be arising, it will warn you by popping up a notification balloon at the bottom-right of the Windows desktop. In case you miss the balloon, Action Center will also appear in your system tray (next to the clock) as a white flag with a red X icon. Click it and you'll see the message, along with a link to open the main Action Center interface. And if it's a warning you're not interested in, you can simply click to disable it.

Don't go disabling things willy-nilly, though: Action Center could be the only warning you receive of potentially serious problems such as virus infections or backup failures.

You don't need to keep checking Action Center, as it flags up any issues in the system tray.

WORRIED ABOUT VIRUSES? THERE'S NO NEED – WINDOWS 8'S BUILT-IN
WINDOWS DEFENDER SYSTEM CAN STOP MOST OF THEM IN THEIR TRACKS

Windows Defender

Microsoft is constantly working to improve Windows' security features, but viruses sadly remain a fact of computing life. To be precise, it's not only viruses that are the problem, but all types of unwanted software, known collectively as "malware".

It's long been understood that the best defence against malware is dedicated security software that can forensically examine every file that's opened on your system, compare it to a vast database of known malware, and automatically block it if it's found to be malicious. Companies such as AVG, Kaspersky, McAfee and Norton have made their names producing this sort of software, and we'll discuss their wares in more detail later in this chapter. But now Windows 8 comes with its own powerful anti-malware program, called Windows Defender, built right into the operating system.

If you've used Microsoft's free Security Essentials program, you may quickly recognise that Defender is basically the same thing under a new name. Under normal circumstances, however, you won't see Windows Defender

at all, as it spends most of its time hidden away in the background; it doesn't even put an icon in the system tray next to the desktop clock. Defender makes itself known only when you try to download or access an untrusted file: then, an unobtrusive notification tile appears at the top right of the screen to let you know that malware has been found and is being dealt with. You can ignore this and leave Defender to do its thing automatically, or click on this tile to be taken to the main Windows Defender interface and examine the details of what it's discovered.

USING WINDOWS DEFENDER Compared to most third-party security suites, Windows Defender is a very limited tool, but it covers the basics admirably. You can access its interface by simply typing "defender" on the Windows 8 Start screen. When the interface appears, you'll see a coloured bar along the top showing the protection status of your PC, along with a friendly graphic showing the same thing. If your protection is turned off, or your database is out of date, it really is impossible to miss: there will be big red warnings

Tip

Confusingly, Microsoft supplies a different program called Windows Defender with Windows 7. This detects only a specific type of malware (known as spyware), so on its own it provides only very limited protection. Don't worry, though: Windows Defender in Windows 8 is a true all-rounder.

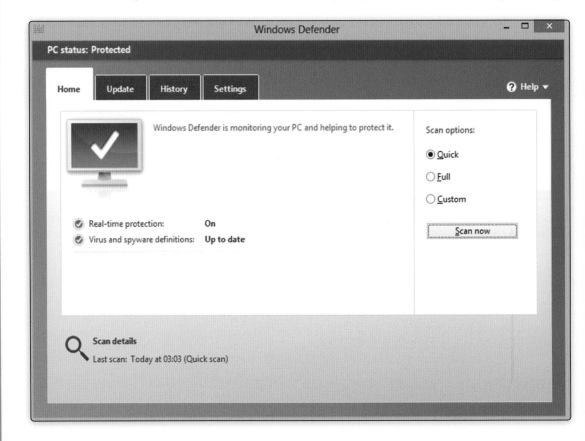

The Windows Defender interface makes it simple to find out what threats it's found on your system.

HOW LONG?
Scanning takes place in the background, so you should notice no interruption at all.

HOW HARD?
Windows Defender is preinstalled, so there's nothing for you to do – just relax, safe in the knowledge that you're protected!

all over the interface, not to mention alerts from Action Center (see p118).

Below the status bar you'll see four tabs, from which Defender's settings can be accessed. From the Home tab you can run a quick scan or a full scan by selecting the appropriate button and clicking "Scan now". You can also set up a custom scan to check specific drives or directories.

The second tab is labelled Update. It's important to keep your security software updated, as new types of malware emerge every day. Windows Defender gets its updates via Windows Update (see p114), which means most of us will never have to think about it. However, if you've disabled automatic Windows Updates, your security database is in danger of falling behind. On the Update tab you can see when Security Essentials was last updated, and launch an immediate update.

The third tab, History, lets you keep track of items that have been detected and quarantined, or whitelisted by you. Finally, the Settings tab is where you'll find most of Defender's technical options, divided into categories in the left-hand pane. Here you can turn real-time protection on or off, opt to exclude certain types of file and process from scanning, and decide what happens to files that are identified as dangerous and quarantined. You can also decide whether to join the Microsoft Active Protection Service (MAPS), which shares information about detected suspicious items to help improve malware detection.

The one thing you won't find is a way to set up a periodic scan of your whole system. But don't panic: the feature is available via a new Windows 8 feature called Automatic Maintenance. By default, this is configured to scan your system for malware at three o'clock each morning, as well as checking for updates and performing system diagnostics. If you want to change the timing of these services, you can do so by opening the Action Center and clicking to configure Automatic Maintenance.

IS DEFENDER GOOD ENOUGH? In *PC Pro* magazine's recent independent security software tests, Windows Defender protected a test PC against 92% of malware of all kinds – suggesting that, for the vast majority of malware attacks, it should be sharp enough to save your bacon. And it's certainly unobtrusive, to the point you can entirely forget it's there, until you need it.

However, commercial anti-malware packages do still have their advantages. Many of them achieved even higher detection rates in *PC Pro*'s lab tests, with several nudging 100%. What's more, paid-for packages are typically much more configurable, and provide additional features such as protection against malicious and junk emails, a "game mode" that prevents interruptions while you're playing games, and tools to help ensure your personal data can't be spied on or stolen. If you prefer to take a more hands-on approach to security, or are willing to pay for extra reassurance, check out p126 for our guide to some of the best major security suites.

For those who like a simple life, though, Windows Defender is a great free extra, and good enough to suggest you don't need to splash out on third-party software.

If Windows Defender spots anything suspicious, it lets you know by popping up an unobtrusive notification tile.

 NOT ALL ATTACKS COME FROM WEBSITES AND DODGY DOWNLOADS. A FIREWALL ENSURES WORMS AND HACKERS CAN'T CONNECT TO YOUR PC

Windows Firewall

A firewall is a piece of software that prevents unwanted people and programs from connecting to your computer over the internet. This protects you against hackers and a particular nasty sort of malware called worms, which spread across networks.

A firewall can also prevent programs on your PC from opening outbound connections, or warn you when this happens. This is sensible because if a new program appears unexpectedly on your system and starts trying to make network connections, that's malware-like behaviour, and could indicate that your computer has contracted an infection that needs removing.

Clearly, a good firewall is an important aspect of overall security, and many security suites come with built-in firewalls (we'll discuss this on the following pages). You don't necessarily need to invest in one of these packages, though, because Windows 8 comes with its own built-in firewall. As with Windows Defender, you may not have realised this firewall is protecting you, as it's designed not to interfere with typical online activities such as browsing the web and sharing files – and when it does detect a suspicious attempt to connect to your PC, the connection is silently blocked. However, to keep yourself as safe as possible, it's a good idea to understand a bit about how the Windows Firewall works and how to configure it.

WHERE ARE YOU? When you connect to a new network in Windows 8, you'll be asked whether or not you want to turn on sharing between PCs on that network. If you're using a trusted network at home or in the office, you can say yes to this, and you'll immediately be able to connect to shared drives and other devices on that network. If you're somewhere like an internet café or an airport, we recommend that you say no: this tells the firewall to lock down sharing features, so unknown characters can't connect to your PC and start browsing your personal files. If you want to change this setting later, click on the network icon in the system tray to make the Networks pane appear, then right-click on the network you want to change and select "Turn sharing on or off".

Whichever option you choose, you'll get an alert if a program tries to open a network connection in a suspicious way. If it's a program you recognise and trust, it's normally okay to allow this; if it's a program you don't even remember installing, we suggest you deny it and scan your system for malware.

FIREWALL CONTROLS In some cases, a firewall can interfere with a legitimate program, such as an online game or a network tool. If something isn't working as it should, you can try manually allowing it through the firewall.

Tip

Some third-party firewalls have a "learning mode" that permits all internet access for a limited time, to learn what sort of network activity is "normal" for your PC based on what happens during this period. It's a clever compromise, but it's obviously vital that no malware is running during the learning period.

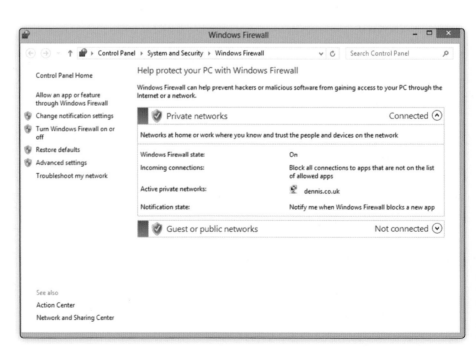

You can change Windows Firewall's settings in the Control Panel's System and Security options.

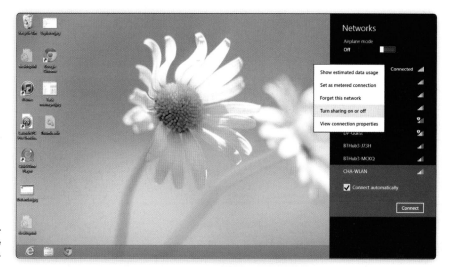

Right: Turn sharing on or off in the Networks pane in the system tray.

Left: It's advisable to turn off sharing in public places such as internet cafés and Wi-Fi hotspots.

HOW LONG?
The firewall runs automatically, and you won't even notice it's there.

HOW HARD?
The firewall is preconfigured, and it's fairly easy to make adjustments if you need to.

You can access Windows 8's Firewall controls by searching Settings for "firewall". You'll see several options. To grant a program network access, the option you want is called "Allow an app through Windows Firewall". Open this and you'll see a long list of applications and features installed on your system, along with details of whether they're allowed to communicate over private and public networks (that is, networks on which sharing is allowed, and networks on which it's restricted). If you want to change the settings for any of them, click "Change settings", then adjust your options. If the application you see isn't listed, click "Allow another app..." to browse a complete list of registered applications installed on your PC.

If you want to take more control, you can open the main Firewall settings window, which you can find by searching for "Windows Firewall" from the Start screen, or clicking on System and Security from the Control Panel.

From here you have numerous options. Clicking "Change notification settings" doesn't only affect how often Windows Firewall alerts you, it also lets you set how paranoid the firewall should be on private and public

networks. "Block all incoming connections, including those in the list of allowed apps" means your internet access is effectively shut off. At the other extreme you can switch off Windows Firewall altogether using the radio button at the bottom. You'll then be inundated with warnings (although you can disable them) until you turn it back on.

Experts can click on Advanced settings to access a much more detailed view, allowing you to edit connection rules in far greater detail. For example, you can allow a connection only if it's secure, and you can define precisely what you mean by secure. You can selectively grant network access to applications depending on which user is logged in, and specify different rules for outbound and inbound traffic. If all this sounds alarmingly complex, don't worry; for most users this level of control isn't necessary and the Windows Firewall usually picks a sensible balance between security and flexibility by default.

Lastly, if you ever get into a mess, you can always select "Restore defaults" to revert the Windows Firewall back to its original settings – so don't be afraid to experiment.

WINDOWS' SIMPLE APPROVAL SYSTEM MAY NOT LOOK VERY SOPHISTICATED, BUT IT'S A VALUABLE DEFENCE AGAINST HACKER ATTACKS

User Account Control

User Account Control (UAC for short) is a system built into Windows that prevents software from making important changes to your system without your approval. The principal idea, of course, is to prevent malware from infiltrating your system, but it can also provide a helpful confirmation stage to legitimate operations too.

There's no denying that, in some quarters, UAC has a bad reputation. This is because when the system was first introduced in Windows Vista it popped up far too often, nagging users to confirm even minor actions such as changing the date. Understandably, many people simply turned it off, leaving themselves completely exposed, without any of the protection UAC was designed to provide.

Happily, the updated implementations of UAC that have since appeared in Windows 7 and now in Windows 8 are much improved. Like all the best security tools – indeed, like Windows Defender and Windows Firewall – UAC is something you'll rarely see, especially if you've bought a PC that's preinstalled with Windows 8 and a suite of applications. In your first few days with the operating system you'll probably run into it half a dozen times, as you install applications and customise your desktop, but after that you'll rarely see a UAC requester without a good reason.

ADMINISTRATOR ACCOUNTS At first glance, UAC may not appear to have anything to do with user accounts: when you encounter it, it will probably manifest simply as a box on a dimmed background, asking you to authorise a named program to make changes to your computer. Indeed, this may also seem like a rather weak sort of protection, which does very little to prevent you from accidentally making disastrous changes.

If you think that, however, it's because you're running Windows as an Administrator. These privileged types see simple Yes and No options in their UAC requesters. When a user logged in with a standard account tries to do something that's protected by UAC – such as installing a new application, or changing important Windows settings – they'll see a requester prompting them to enter an Administrator password. Without this password, the operation can't be completed. In other words, the operation needs permission from an authorised user account.

(The dimmed screen has a reason, too: it indicates that background applications are temporarily locked out, so only people – and not programs – can approve UAC requests.)

It's good practice with Windows to have all the users of your PC – including yourself – log in with standard accounts. This way, it's harder for you to make system-level changes by accident. Thanks to the way UAC works, however, you can still change settings if you wish to, simply by maintaining a separate Administrator account and providing its password when required. Using a standard account also means that if you leave your PC accidentally logged in, other users can't come along and take advantage.

Giving standard accounts to others also makes it possible to manage your network. For example, if you want to use Family Safety to protect your children, standard accounts are a must. You can't apply restrictions to an Administrator account, since by definition an Administrator could simply undo them again.

DISABLING UAC If you regularly find UAC warning boxes popping up and you find the intrusions annoying, you can turn them off. We certainly don't recommend this, but it's easy enough to do. Simply search from the Start screen for "UAC" to find the relevant Control Panel item listed under Settings. You'll see a settings window open with a single slider bar, with options ranging from "Always notify" at the top, down to "Never notify" at the bottom. If you want, you can drag the slider down by just one notch to disable screen dimming, although frankly there's no benefit to doing so.

To disable UAC entirely, drag the slide bar down to its lowest position and click OK. The screen will dim one last time and you'll be asked if you really want to do such a thing. If your PC has only recently booted, your new settings may take effect immediately; normally, though, you'll have to restart your PC to be rid of UAC.

Without UAC, you can still use the different privileges of Administrator and standard accounts to protect your system, ensuring other users log in with standard

Tip

◢ UAC shows different graphical prompts depending on what an application or user is trying to do. The quartered shield indicates that a Windows feature is trying to start. A question mark indicates an application that isn't part of Windows but has a valid digital signature. An orange shield with an exclamation mark relates to an unknown program, and a red shield means Administrator access is needed.

User Account Control will ask your permission before allowing a program to make changes to your computer.

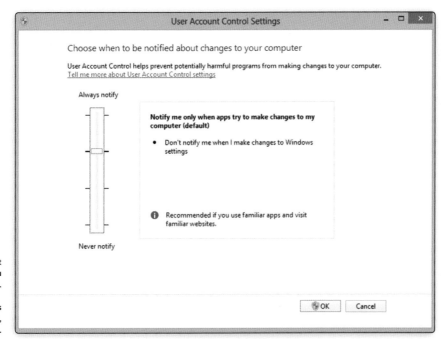

User Account Control Settings

Choose when to be notified about changes to your computer

User Account Control helps prevent potentially harmful programs from making changes to your computer.
Tell me more about User Account Control settings

Always notify

Notify me only when apps try to make changes to my computer (default)

- Don't notify me when I make changes to Windows settings

ℹ Recommended if you use familiar apps and visit familiar websites.

Never notify

OK   Cancel

Right: It's easy to adjust how often UAC notifies you of any changes.

Below: UAC notifications dim the rest of the screen, so you can't miss them.

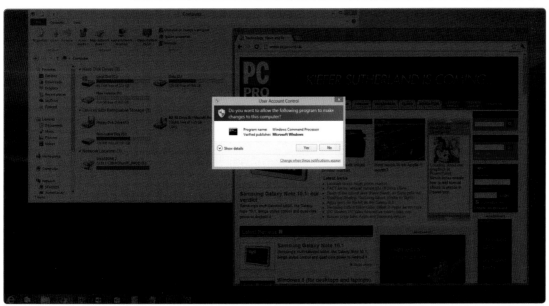

HOW LONG?
UAC is set up by default, and you'll barely notice it running.

HOW HARD?
Just keep your wits about you and don't blindly accept any unexpected requesters.

accounts and doing so yourself whenever you know you won't need to change system settings or install software. But you'll lose that extra confirmation step of UAC when running as Administrator.

Standard users – including you, when you're logged in as such – have it worse. When they try to carry out a task that's normally protected by UAC, they won't be prompted to provide a password: instead they'll just see a message saying they "must be a computer administrator" to perform this task. They (or you) will have to save their work, log out and log back in as an Administrator. Depending on how you use your PC, this may well prove to be more hassle than putting up with UAC in the first place.

User Account Control

Do you want to allow the following program to make changes to this computer?

Program name: Dropbox 1.4.12 Installer
Verified publisher: **Dropbox**
File origin: Hard drive on this computer

ⓥ Show details   Yes   No

Change when these notifications appear

You can allow programs to make changes to your PC only if you're logged in as an Administrator.

IF YOU'RE NOT CONVINCED BY WHAT'S BUILT INTO WINDOWS, THERE ARE PLENTY OF ALTERNATIVES OUT THERE. HERE ARE SOME OF THE BEST

Third-party security software

If Windows Defender doesn't satisfy you, there are plenty of more sophisticated third-party alternatives – commonly referred to as "security suites", on account of their bringing together a range of different security tools.

There are numerous advantages to third-party security suites. One is the use of what's called "cloud protection", which uses a central online database to detect malware, so that as soon as a new threat is created, all users are immediately protected.

Many security suites also include their own firewall, replacing the one included with Windows 8. Some of these are much "noisier" than the Windows one: that might sound like a bad thing, but it means the software will make fewer assumptions about which connections are desirable and which aren't. For technical users, this may be preferable. A third-party firewall may also allow you to create more complex rules – for example, you might decide that a certain program is allowed to access the internet only via a certain port when connected to a certain type of network.

Another feature typically found in many third-party suites is a web-scanning module, which warns you whenever you visit a web page that's known to harbour dangerous code or one that appears to be a scam. This might appear as a toolbar in your browser, showing alerts of various colours as you browse. A green light would mean that the site has been verified as safe, and you can browse and download files with confidence, whereas a red light would indicate that you were visiting a site that was known to be dangerous.

Some scanners give you an earlier warning by placing safety ratings next to your results in web search engines such as Google and Bing – an approach called "link scanning". For example, if you're searching for "free games", you'll be able to see at a glance which sites have a good reputation and which have been associated with malware. There's no need to click the links to expose dangerous sites – you can simply skip right over them. A few security suites (such as Norton Internet Security; see below) take this idea further and also provide trust information for online shopping sites, so, for example, you can see at a glance what type of security an online store uses and what its reputation is.

Tip

◢ Almost all security suites are offered on a time-limited trial basis, so if you can't decide which suite to go for, download a trial and see what you think. Some suites are also offered in a range of editions, containing different features at different prices, so check your options before you buy.

Third-party security software includes a raft of extra features, and packages such as AVG Anti-Virus won't cost you a penny.

Bitdefender's features include Wi-Fi network monitoring and free plug-ins to protect you from potentially dangerous content on Twitter and Facebook.

HOW LONG?
Downloading, installing and performing an initial scan takes a little while, but things are automatic after that.

HOW HARD?
Installing third-party security software needn't be hard, but some packages are designed for more technical users.

At the extreme end, some third-party security suites provide a "safe browser" – that is, a web browser that's designed to provide better security than a regular one, so you can visit unknown sites with confidence. This means, for example, that you might be asked to provide explicit permission when a site wants to store a cookie on your PC, or when it wants to show an embedded Flash video, which can compromise your PC's security.

EXTRA TOOLS AND SETTINGS In addition to these mainstream features, some third-party packages offer extra tools and settings, to provide extra protection or convenience – and to set themselves apart from the pack. For example, some software monitors all the computers and devices on your network, and alerts you whenever anything new connects, in case it's an unauthorised intruder.

Some programs feature a silent "game mode" or "movie mode", suppressing alerts when they detect that you're using an application with a full-screen view. Some software may also dial back its CPU and network usage, so as not to interfere if you're playing a game. A "sandbox" feature lets you find out what a program does without giving it full access to your system, or putting your personal information at risk.

You may also see features designed to provide security for your data. A personal information monitor might prevent certain pieces of information (such as credit card numbers) from being sent from your PC out on to the internet. Some security software includes encryption functions that you can use to ensure that even if someone gets hold of your sensitive information, they will be unable to read it without knowing your secure password. A security suite might include so-called "shredding" tools that completely wipe selected files from the disk, ensuring they can't be recovered.

DOWNSIDES TO SECURITY SOFTWARE There are a few possible catches to using this type of software. Not all security software costs money, but if you want the best features and maximum protection, you'll have to look to a commercial package. This isn't just a one-off cost; in order to provide you with continuous protection against the latest threats, all security software needs regular updates, so you're effectively buying a service. Most internet security software comes with a one-year subscription, after which you'll have to pay again to keep receiving updates.

We should also mention security software's impact on performance. It's sometimes claimed that antivirus software will slow your PC to a crawl: this is a myth, but checking files for malware does take some time, and it does use up some memory.

The final problem is the sheer range of choice on offer. There are so many different security suites available, each with its own feature list and strengths and weaknesses, that choosing one can be very difficult. To make your decision easier, we've looked at the strengths and weaknesses of the major titles.

AVG ANTI-VIRUS AVG Anti-Virus is a popular third-party security program, not least because it's free. It also has a well-deserved reputation for effectiveness: in *PC Pro*'s tests, it achieved an impressive 98% malware protection score, significantly higher than the 92% managed by Windows Defender. The software includes a few useful features that Security Essentials lacks, such as a web-protection module (called LinkScanner) that integrates with your web browser and adds warnings to your web search results, helping you steer clear of dangerous pages. Be warned, however, that this free program is supported by advertising: while using it, you'll see plenty of adverts for the company's commercial products.

8
Security

BITDEFENDER INTERNET SECURITY Bitdefender Internet Security has a moody, dark interface, and plenty of features, including web protection, Wi-Fi network monitoring and optional free plug-ins to protect you from potentially dangerous content on Twitter and Facebook. It also includes a safe browser, a scanner that finds unpatched programs on your system and privacy and encryption tools. But don't be daunted: it's actually a very easy security suite to use, thanks to its innovative "Auto Pilot" mode. When this is switched on, Bitdefender handles everything, without interrupting you at all. If you want more control, simply switch it off and you can deal with firewall requests and malware detection events yourself. In *PC Pro*'s tests it achieved a perfect 100% score, making it an appealing option for both notices and expert users alike.

ESET SMART SECURITY Smart Security's main interface is so clean and minimal that you might take it for a bare-bones program. Yet beneath that super-simple front-end you'll find all the important security suite features, including a firewall, a web protection module and parental controls. Indeed, there's plenty here to appeal to technical users: when malware is found, a detailed alert gives you all the information you need to decide what to do, and the firewall gives technical information about what's happening, helping expert users to keep track of network events.

It's also a highly efficacious malware scanner: in *PC Pro*'s tests, Smart Security gave protection against 100% of malware samples while allowing 95% of legitimate applications to run without a murmur.

F-SECURE INTERNET SECURITY F-Secure's security suite uses a malware detection engine licensed from Bitdefender, so it was no surprise to see another perfect 100% malware

protection score in *PC Pro*'s tests. In use it provides a decent amount of technical information and options for advanced users, with firewall activity alerts providing plenty of detail about potentially dangerous events, including the network systems and ports involved. The suite also features an Online Safety module, where you can set up web restrictions for your children and online protection for yourself, although the quirky blue, white and green interface won't be to everybody's taste.

KASPERSKY INTERNET SECURITY Moscow-based Kaspersky Lab offers not only antivirus scanning but a wide range of tools, including sandbox technology and a virtual keyboard, for entering passwords undetected by trojans. Kaspersky Internet Security tends to put the user in control, meaning you can expect to see more pop-ups and requesters than with some other software; less experienced users may find this daunting, although the interface is kept as simple as possible. In *PC Pro*'s malware tests, the software delivered a clean sweep. And when Kaspersky Internet Security detects a piece of malware, it doesn't keep quiet. The pop-up notification gives you a detailed explanation of what's going on and what action it's taken. You can click the "Details..." link for yet more information about the threat. For more advanced users, it's a compelling choice.

McAFEE INTERNET SECURITY McAfee is now owned by chip manufacturer Intel, but it has no special virus-detecting powers: sad to say, it protected against only 52% of malware samples in *PC Pro*'s tests. Despite that, it sports an impressive range of features, including a home network scanner, a file shredder, a built-in web-scanning module and even an online backup system. What's more, the package price includes 1GB of online backup – enough

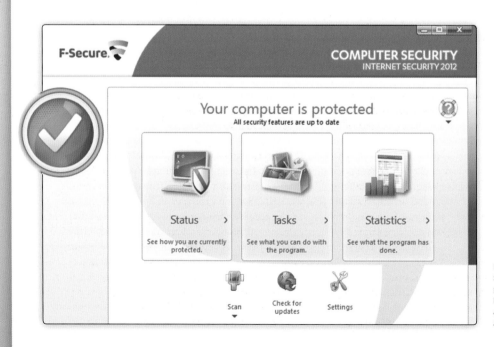

F-Secure Internet Security includes plenty of detailed information as well as lots of options for advanced users.

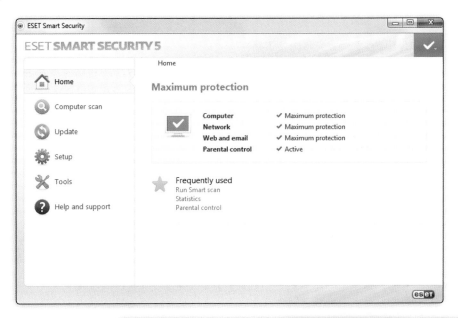

Beneath Eset Smart Security's simple interface are some powerful anti-malware features.

Kaspersky Internet Security provides a wide range of additional tools, such as sandbox technology and a virtual keyboard.

FAQ

Q: Is it better to buy a boxed copy of a security suite, or to download it directly from the publisher's website?

A: Security software updates itself automatically, so whichever you choose you'll be protected against the latest threats. However, prices can differ considerably between high-street shops, online stores such as Amazon and publisher websites, so shop around before making a purchase. The same applies when it's time to renew: don't just accept the default renewal offer. It may be much cheaper to buy a new boxed copy than to extend your existing licence for another year.

to accommodate your most important documents and spreadsheets. It's for you to decide whether McAfee's excellent range of features makes up for that uncertain anti-malware performance.

NORTON INTERNET SECURITY Norton is one of the best-known names in the security business. Its early products earned an unenviable reputation for being bloated and intrusive, but the latest version of Norton Internet Security makes modest demands on your system, especially when you consider it has a feature list as long as your arm. Dig into the interface and you'll find a network scanner, a password manager, web protection and cloud-based features to ensure up-to-the-second protection. The sheer wealth of features on offer can be overwhelming, and the interface isn't as clearly organised as you might hope. However,

Norton achieved 96% score in *PC Pro*'s malware protection tests, showing that it's a very capable package that deserves a place on your shortlist.

TREND MICRO TITANIUM INTERNET SECURITY Trend Micro's security suite is as impenetrable as its name: in *PC Pro*'s malware tests it blocked 100% of malware samples tested. Unusually, the suite doesn't include a third-party firewall, relying instead on the standard Windows Firewall, but that helps keep things simple. Titanium Internet Security offers all the other major features you'd expect from a security suite, plus a welcome Security Report view that breaks down the different types of threat found in an accessible format, so you can easily see what the software is doing for you. The cherry on top is a generous 2GB of online backup, via the company's SafeSync package, included in the price.

IN THIS CHAPTER

132 Touchscreen gestures
Using Windows 8 on a tablet is about more than just tapping and swiping. There's a whole world of gestures to help you get around quickly.

134 Mastering the onscreen keyboard
Windows 8 works well on a tablet because the keyboard is so good. We show you how it works and unveil some hidden shortcuts.

136 Handwriting recognition
You don't have to stick with a keyboard for entering text; Windows 8's brilliant handwriting lets you digitise your scrawl as well.

9
Windows 8 on tablets

WINDOWS 8 ON T

Microsoft has completely revamped the Windows interface in its biggest overhaul since Windows 95. The force behind that change is the emergent popularity of tablets. In this chapter, we'll show you how the new look works on the devices it was designed for. You'll discover how to get around the front-end quickly using a selection of swipes, taps and Microsoft's ingenious

ABLETS

edge gestures. We'll unveil the power of the Windows 8 touch keyboard, which allows you to type emails and documents almost as quickly as on a laptop or desktop keyboard. And we'll show you how Microsoft's superlative handwriting recognition technology, coupled with a stylus and digitiser pen, takes text entry to the next level.

9

Windows 8 on tablets

WINDOWS 8 INTRODUCES AN ARRAY OF NEW GESTURE CONTROLS. IT'S TIME TO BECOME A MASTER AT USING WINDOWS WITH YOUR FINGERS

Touchscreen gestures

There's little doubt that Windows 8 brings with it the most radical interface overhaul Microsoft has ever undertaken, and that dramatic change is all about making Windows easier to use on touchscreen devices – primarily tablets.

The new-look Windows 8 introduces live tiles – square icons that are large enough to be tapped with a finger. There's a selection of core apps that have been designed specifically for tablets and touchscreen PCs, and a Windows Store packed with many more.

There's also a touch-friendly new way of protecting your Windows user account, and keeping your PC or tablet safe from unwanted eyes. Picture passwords involve having to tap points and draw lines or circles in a set way on a personal photograph to gain access to your Windows 8 user account – see p40 for more.

CORE GESTURES Let's return to the basics, however, since to get the most out of Windows 8 as a touchscreen user, it's vital to learn the core gestures. Touch gestures are special finger swipes used to carry out key navigational tasks. The most basic touch gesture of all, and one you're invariably already familiar with from using a smartphone, is the single finger swipe.

On the Windows 8 Start screen, single-finger swipes happen horizontally. Place your finger on the screen and swipe or flick it left or right, and the Live tiles of the Start screen will whizz quickly and smoothly past.

In other applications, though, it's different. In Internet Explorer 10, for instance, a swipe left or right takes you back or forwards a page in your browsing history.

In menus, web pages, and the Windows 8 desktop, the main form of scrolling is by using up and down gestures, and if you're zoomed into a web page or picture, you can use a single-finger drag in any direction to move around to different parts of it.

Another key gesture is the pinch. Pioneered and popularised by Apple on the iPhone, this allows you to zoom in and out. In a web browser or while viewing a photo, you can use the zoom-in pinch to quickly hone in on difficult-to-read text or to make a tiny link easier to tap accurately. Simply start with two fingers together, place them on the screen and quickly pull them apart.

A zoom-out pinch, meanwhile, allows you to zoom out, or pull back to get a quick overview of pictures or web pages. You can also use pinch zoom to bring up a "helicopter view" of your Windows 8 Start screen. Just pinch your fingers together on the Start screen and the view zooms right out; to zoom back in to a particular region, just pinch zoom on the area or tap it.

EDGE SWIPES These simple gestures are designed to be a core part of the Windows 8 experience for touchscreen users, but there are also a handful of less obvious gestures that are still worth knowing. They're called "edge swipes", and are performed by placing a finger on the border surrounding the screen and dragging it towards the centre.

The one you'll use the most is the swipe in from the right-hand edge of the screen. This brings up the Charms menu, which houses shortcuts to Windows 8's search facility, the Start screen, plus Devices, Settings and Share menus. The Charms swipe is a global command – in other words, it will bring up the Charms menu on-screen regardless of what you're doing at the time.

That isn't the case for the next gesture in our list, however. The swipe in from the top or bottom of the screen is context-sensitive, and will achieve different results depending on where you are at the time. In Internet Explorer 10, for instance, performing this gesture will cause the open tabs and address bar to appear on-screen; on the Windows Start screen, meanwhile, it will bring up a bar containing a single button on it for

Tip

It's not only the new Windows Start screen that responds to touch controls, the traditional Windows desktop and applications do too. However, seeing that neither the desktop nor the vast majority of desktop apps were designed to be prodded with fingers, we suggest you keep a mouse and keyboard handy if you plan to work on the desktop.

Top: swipe in from the left side of the screen to scroll through the open apps on your PC. Bottom: a quick swipe from the left edge and back again opens a tray of open apps to choose from.

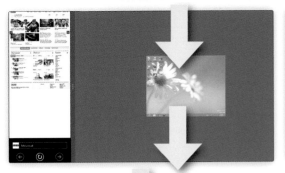

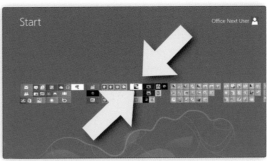

displaying a full list of all your apps; on the Windows desktop, however, it does nothing at all.

Choose to lengthen the top-down swipe and keep your finger held against the screen, and things change yet again, allowing you to position the current app to the left or right of Windows 8's split-screen view, or close it by continuing the swipe off the bottom of the display.

That one is another global command, as is our final gesture: swiping in from the left edge of the screen. If you have many apps open at once, a quick, short flick of the finger switches you to the next one in the list. Keep flicking and the process of navigating your way through even long lists of apps becomes incredibly easy; it's effectively a fancy version of the classic Windows keyboard shortcut, Alt-Tab.

Again, it doesn't end there. Keep your finger on the screen after a left-edge swipe and two more options

Multitouch touchpads

Once you've learned the main gestures, Windows 8 is a quick, slick operating system to get around – but what about laptops without touchscreens? Well, those with multitouch touchpads work just as well, as the gestures are very similar.

In fact, if you imagine your laptop touchpad is a small touchscreen, you'll be halfway there: swipes from the left, right, top and bottom all work the same as edge swipes on a touchscreen. The only major difference is how single-finger swipes are recreated: to scroll up and down, and pan left and right in web pages and pictures, you push up, down, left and right with two fingers instead of one.

become available. You can reposition the swiped-in application to take up the left or right side of a split-screen view or, by pulling your finger back over to the left edge, bring up the task switcher menu that displays thumbnails of the six apps you've used most recently.

WINDOWS 8 COMES WITH A VARIETY OF ONSCREEN KEYBOARD OPTIONS: WE SHOW YOU HOW TO ACCESS THE DIFFERENT VERSIONS AND WHAT THEY OFFER

Mastering the onscreen keyboard

We've already seen how gestures help you get around in Windows 8. But what about entering text? Typing in web addresses, keywords for web searches, writing emails and even longer tranches of text on a tablet wouldn't be possible without a decent onscreen keyboard, and that's precisely what Windows 8 offers.

On a tablet, the onscreen keyboard appears automatically when you tap in an editable text field – the password box on the Lock screen, the Windows 8 Search, or the body of an email, for example. If you're using an older application on the Windows 8 desktop, you'll need to launch the keyboard manually after tapping on a document, using the keyboard launch button on the right-hand side of the taskbar at the bottom of the screen.

Once you've started typing, you'll find the Windows 8 virtual keyboard almost as quick as a physical one. The keys are highly responsive, and in the standard layout they're large and easy to press. In fact, the Windows 8 keyboard behaves just like a physical one in many ways: to type a capital letter, hold down Shift and press a key; to cut, copy and paste, use Ctrl-X, C and V; to highlight text, hold the Shift key and tap or hold the left or right cursor keys.

KEYBOARD BASICS There are some differences, though. In order to make the keyboard so usable, Microsoft has removed many of the keys you might expect to see on a standard physical keyboard. Take a close look and you'll see the number key top row and symbols such as the colon, semicolon and brackets aren't there.

To access these and others from the standard keyboard layout it is a simple case of tapping the &123 key in the bottom-left corner of the keyboard. This brings up a special layout with a number pad to the right and a selection of commonly used symbols on a pad to the left. If the symbol you need isn't listed, tapping the small arrow just above the &123 key brings up another symbol panel containing less commonly used symbols.

There are other clever features at work here. The keyboard will notice when you mis-type some words and correct them. It's a subtle system and won't correct massive mistakes such as the autocorrect system on a smartphone might, but it will correct obvious typos, such as dropping in apostrophes and changing 'teh' to 'the', for example.

Keep an eye out, too, for word suggestions, which can help you enter long words more quickly. These "suggestions" appear in a rectangular box below text as you type, and the system learns as it goes. If you use the word "lighthouse" frequently in one piece of writing, for example, by the time you reach the end of your piece, the keyboard will be predicting the word by the time you've typed "li".

SPECIAL CHARACTERS AND ALTERNATIVE LAYOUTS There are limitations to a touchscreen keyboard, most notably space, but it can be more flexible in other ways. Nowhere is this more obvious than when typing special characters, such as accented letters. With a physical keyboard typing an accented é can be a slow and painful process. You have to pick up your mouse, go to the Insert menu (in Word), then

Tip

Take your time to learn how to quickly enter the core punctuation symbols. It's much quicker to swipe left and right from the question mark than it is to switch to the full symbol and number layout, and will save you a lot of time in the long run.

Another advantage of touch keyboards is that you can switch to an entirely different layout at the touch of a button. In Windows 8 there are

<u>there</u> are alternative keyboard layouts you can use, if you can't stand having to flick over to the &123 keyboard to access the numbers. In the bottom right-hand corner of the keyboard

HOW LONG?
If you know how to use a physical keyboard, getting used to Windows 8's touch keyboard should take only a minute or two.

HOW HARD?
Using the touch keyboard is easy – it's just like using a laptop or desktop keyboard.

Top: Windows 8's touchscreen keyboard is ideal for use on tablets, with large, easy-to-tap keys and a simplified layout.

Middle: The split keyboard is designed to let you type with your thumbs while holding a tablet in two hands. The letters and common symbols are clustered close to the edges of the screen, with numbers in the centre.

Bottom: Press and hold a letter key, and a selection of related characters or symbols will appear. You can also press and swipe in the direction of the character you want to insert it more quickly.

pick what you need from the symbol menu (or remember a keyboard shortcut). With a Windows 8 tablet that same letter can be inserted by simply holding down the e on the touch keyboard until a menu pops up with related special characters, then dragging a finger to the é.

This works not only for letters, but also for symbols. Hold down the ? key on the main keyboard, and a cluster of related symbols will appear, giving quick access to !, @, left and right brackets and more. An even quicker way to enter these symbols is to simply hit the key and drag your finger in the direction of that symbol. A left and right drag on the ? key, for instance, inserts open and close brackets.

With touch keyboards you can also switch to a different layout at the touch of a button. Windows 8 offers you two alternatives as standard: the first is laid out like a physical keyboard, complete with a row of numbers along the top and all the standard symbols. The other is a thumb keyboard for when you're holding the tablet in two hands. In this version the keyboard is split in half, with small clusters of keys placed within easy reach of the thumbs on each side of the screen.

Changing the way keyboards behave

Generally we'd advise you to leave the Windows 8 onscreen keyboard in its default settings. It works very well indeed, and even the autocorrect isn't too aggressive, gently suggesting alternatives instead of distractingly shoving suggestions in your face.

However, if you find the suggestions it comes up with are starting to get on your nerves, they can be switched off, along with a number of other potentially annoying default settings, such as the option to insert spaces automatically after inserting a word from the suggestions, and capitalising letters at the beginning of sentences.

9
Windows 8 on tablets

Handwriting recognition

It's odd to think that until relatively recently, computers haven't been clever enough to cope with the most ancient form of written communication. Only now, with the advent of powerful touchscreen tablets and the arrival of Windows 8, is it becoming a major form of digital input.

It isn't the first time handwriting recognition has been included as a feature in Windows. In fact, Microsoft introduced the technology two versions ago in Windows Vista with the arrival of the touch input panel, then refined it for Windows 7, improving accuracy and offering broader language support.

It has always been an accurate system, capable of turning even the most unintelligible scrawl into text for a Word document or your latest Twitter missive. Where Windows 8 is different, however, is that it makes handwriting recognition a major part of the input system.

GETTING STARTED Entering text by writing on your Windows 8 tablet couldn't be simpler. All you do is launch the onscreen keyboard by tapping in any editable field or document, then tap the "Alternative layouts" button in the bottom right-hand corner.

To switch to the handwriting panel, tap the button that looks like a box with a pen across it. The onscreen keyboard will be replaced by a blank box with space for two lines of writing, and a small collection of function buttons to the right. Now simply start writing in the box; Windows 8 will start working its magic as soon as you've finished your first word.

Don't panic if at first the word doesn't appear as you intended. Carry on and finish the sentence, and chances are the input panel will catch up and recognise what you first intended to write. And if the system doesn't get it right, it's easy to make corrections – check out the walkthrough on the opposite page to find out how.

DIFFERENT TYPES OF PEN There are all sorts of ways you can enter text via handwriting in Windows 8. You can use a capacitive stylus – a pen-type implement with a rubber nib that works on any capacitive touchscreen. There's no need for a high-tech approach, though – in fact, you can just use a finger if you like. Either approach will get the job done, but neither represents the most accurate or efficient way of entering text through handwriting recognition.

For best accuracy, you need a tablet equipped with a digitiser – a different form of touch technology than that used to recognise finger taps. It's a system used by specialist graphics tablets for illustration and design work, and while it requires a special pen to work, the result is improved accuracy and a smoother, more natural pen stroke.

Tip

A capacitive touchscreen can't capture fine movement as accurately as a pen and digitiser, so if you're using a finger or a capacitive stylus to enter text via the handwriting recognition panel, bear in mind that you'll need to keep the letters much bigger than normal.

Handwriting recognition in windows 8

It's odd to think that, until very recently, computers haven't been powerful enough to read our handwriting and turn it into text on the page. Yet the potential of harnessing the mighty pen has eluded the broad church of personal computing until recently. With Windows 8's emphasis on tablets and touchscreen tech, however, that's set to change.

Handwriting recognition in Windows 8

Insert

Windows 8 is happy for you to scribble on screen using a stylus or even just a finger.

HOW TO...
DIGITISE YOUR HANDWRITING

1 **DELETING WORDS AND CHARACTERS** Windows 8 uses a combination of handwriting analysis and word completion algorithms to decipher what you've written in the input panel. Most of the time it works beautifully, but no handwriting recognition system is accurate 100% of the time, especially if your handwriting resembles little more than a messy squiggle. When you spot an error, the simplest way to deal with it is to delete it and try again. This is child's play to achieve: simply strike a horizontal line from left to right through the word in question, and it will be removed instantly.

2 **MAKING CORRECTIONS** Many inaccuracies that do come along will see Windows 8 suggesting something that's at least close to what you originally intended to write. In this case, it may be easier to correct the error than to start the word from scratch. To do this, simply tap the word in the input panel, and a list of potential alternatives will pop up above. In our example, we've tried to write "what" but it's been transcribed as "that". A simple tap brings up two alternatives, one of which is the word we were going for. Tap on the right option and the inaccurate word will be replaced.

3 **ADVANCED TECHNIQUES** When you tap on an incorrect word, you'll notice the input panel spreads the word out into individual letters. This comes into its own when the suggested alternatives don't come up with the goods, allowing you to manually correct the word, character by character. If you need to insert an extra character, draw a short vertical line down between two characters and the character will be dropped in. To join two parts of a word together, a "U" symbol under the baseline does the trick. In our example, the word "wrote" was misinterpreted as "vote". To correct it, we drew a line between the "v" and "o" to insert a space, then wrote the letters "w" and "r" in the corresponding spaces, and finally tapped Insert to swap to the new word. And it isn't only text in the input panel that can be corrected in this way. Any word in any document or an editable text field can be corrected in a similar fashion: with the handwriting input panel active, select the word and it will pop up for editing.

4 **IMPROVING YOUR ACCURACY** Windows 8's handwriting recognition feature is remarkably tolerant of terrible script, but it can't work miracles and having to constantly go back and correct errors can be a pain. The answer is to write more clearly, and the first step to doing so is simply to slow down and attempt to form clear, distinguishable letters. Try writing characters separately at first, to learn where the tolerances lie and which letters are proving most problematic, and then slowly progress to joined-up writing. Sticking to the horizontal guidelines helps too. Finally, if you come across a word you use regularly that isn't recognised, you can add it to the handwriting dictionary: simply tap the word in the input panel, then tap the arrow above it and select "Add [your word] to the handwriting dictionary".

HOW LONG?
Getting started takes no time at all, but mastering its quirks is a longer-term undertaking.

HOW HARD?
It's easy to get going, but there are special gestures and penstrokes you'll need to learn.

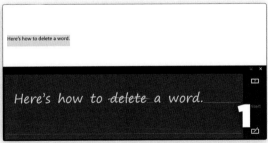

Here's how to delete a word.

Here's how to delete a word.

1

When the system gets close to that you originally intended to write, you can...

That   what

When the system gets close to t h a t

2

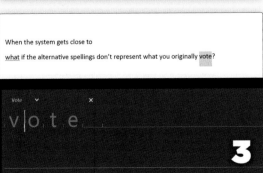

When the system gets close to

what if the alternative spellings don't represent what you originally vote?

Vote

v|o t e

3

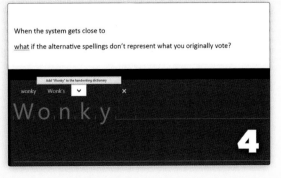

When the system gets close to

what if the alternative spellings don't represent what you originally vote?

Add "Wonky" to the handwriting dictionary

wonky   Wonk's

Wonky

4

IN THIS CHAPTER

140 DVD and Blu-ray playback
Windows no longer offers DVD playback by default. We show you how to get your discs spinning smoothly as before.

142 Windows Media Player
Make the most of your music with the improved Windows Media Player, and find out what's happened to Windows Media Center.

144 Windows 8 and the Xbox 360
Discover how to turn your Windows 8 tablet into a remote control for your Xbox 360 with our guide.

146 Playing games
Find out about the new games available with Windows 8 and how to compete against players from across the globe.

10
Entertainment

ENTERTAINMENT

Windows 8 is much more than a workhorse – it's an all-round entertainer of an operating system, too. With a brand-new breed of games, close compatibility with Microsoft's Xbox 360 console and Windows Media Player, Windows 8 has plenty to keep you amused.

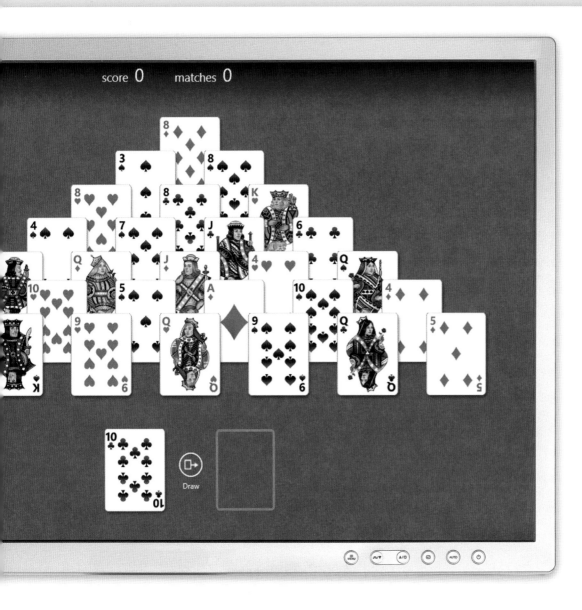

Some of these features are new to Windows 8, others have been revamped. Some – such as DVD playback – have actually been deprecated, but we'll show you how you can make up for the missing features with free, downloadable software.

PLAYING DVDs ON YOUR WINDOWS 8 PC ISN'T AS STRAIGHTFORWARD AS IT WAS IN PREVIOUS VERSIONS. WE EXPLAIN HOW TO PLAY YOUR DISCS

DVD and Blu-ray playback

Those of us with huge DVD movie collections and cupboards full of box sets are well used to popping a disc into our PC or laptop and sitting back and enjoying the show. Sadly, however, things aren't quite that simple in Windows 8, with Microsoft taking the somewhat surprising decision to remove DVD playback functionality from the new operating system.

WHY THE CHANGE? Devices such as tablets and Ultrabooks are now outselling traditional desktop PCs, the majority of which no longer ship with a DVD or Blu-ray drive. For that reason, Microsoft has decided not to include DVD playback by default with Windows 8. Since Microsoft was previously forced to pay a licence fee for DVD codecs (the software that permits DVD playback) for every copy of Windows sold – regardless of whether the user watched DVDs on their system or not – the company decided it was no longer a price worth paying.

HOW TO PLAY DVDs That doesn't mean you won't be able to play DVDs on your Windows 8 PC, however. If you're buying a new PC that comes with a DVD drive, the PC manufacturer will almost certainly have installed player software so that it works out of the box.

If not, you can download and install DVD-playing software yourself. The well-respected VLC Media Player is free to download from www.videolan.org/vlc and offers DVD playback among its many features.

The company behind VLC exploits a loophole in French law that allows it to distribute the DVD codecs without paying a licence fee, and given that it's been operating without legal challenge for many years, it seems unlikely that users will be prevented from using the VLC Media Player any time soon.

HOW TO PLAY BLU-RAY DISCS The situation is a little trickier when it comes to Blu-ray drives and playback. Again, PC manufacturers should supply software with new Blu-ray-equipped PCs, and if you're upgrading a Windows 7 PC to Windows 8 your existing Blu-ray software should survive the transition.

If you're installing a Blu-ray drive yourself in a Windows 8 PC, you'll need to buy specialist player software to watch your movies. Software such as WinDVD Pro (from www.corel.com) or PowerDVD (from www.cyberlink.com) both support Blu-ray playback, and cost around £60. You can download free trials from both companies' websites to test that it works on your PC before you buy.

Tip

◢ Although they were not available at the time of going to press, it's almost certain that movie-streaming services such as LoveFilm and Netflix will release their apps in the Windows Store. They should make it easier for subscribers to access the film libraries on a tablet, and possibly even conventional PCs.

HOW TO...
WATCH FILMS IN WINDOWS 8

 DOWNLOAD MOVIES Downloading films is now more popular than buying a disc, and there are lots of services offering movies over the internet. Microsoft itself offers both downloads and streams (see step 2 below) via the Video app on the Windows 8 Start screen (see p46 for more on this app). Other alternatives include Apple's iTunes Store; download the iTunes software to your PC (from www.apple.com/itunes) and head to the Movies section to see which films are available. Films bought in iTunes can also be transferred to other Apple devices, such as iPads and iPhones.

 STREAMING SERVICES An alternative to downloads for those with decent broadband connections is video streaming. Instead of downloading and storing the film on your PC, streaming services deliver the video "live" over the internet. The two most popular options are Amazon's LoveFilm Instant and Netflix. Both services allow you to stream a wide selection of films and TV shows for a fixed monthly fee, starting from around £5 per month. Films can be streamed to a variety of devices, including PCs, laptops, games consoles and smartphones, but bear in mind that you'll always need to be within reach of a broadband connection to receive the streams – you won't be able to access the services on a plane or train. We wouldn't recommend running a streaming service on a broadband connection with an actual throughput slower than 2Mbits/sec.

 RIP YOUR DVDS If you already have a collection of DVDs and want to watch them on a tablet or laptop without a disc drive, you could "rip" them to a USB stick or the device's hard disk using another computer with a built-in drive. Alas, this process currently constitutes copyright infringement. That said, you're unlikely to face prosecution if you're ripping DVDs for personal use. Upload the ripped DVDs to a file-sharing service, however, and you could face a heavy fine or even imprisonment. One of the most popular ripping programs is HandBrake, a free download from http://handbrake.fr. Note that HandBrake isn't by itself able to rip commercial DVDs. To do this you'll need the DVD43 plug-in (www.dvd43.com), which circumvents the copy protection, and is again in a legal grey area. HandBrake is a little complex, but there are plenty of online guides to show you how to use it. Google "how to rip DVDs with HandBrake".

 DIGITAL COPIES Many DVD and Blu-ray discs come with a so-called Digital Copy (which is bizarre, because films have been nothing but digital since the advent of the DVD). This allows you to transfer a copy of the film to a PC or a portable media player. You'll normally have to enter a one-off activation code online before transferring it. Digital Copies are great, but you may find you have to pay a little extra for them. A new breed of Digital Copy is called UltraViolet Copy, and isn't compatible with Apple's iTunes or its devices.

HOW LONG?
It should take only a few minutes to download and install VLC Media Player and reactivate DVD playback.

HOW HARD?
Microsoft has made it more difficult to watch DVDs in Windows, but the workarounds are not tricky.

10

Entertainment

Windows Media Player

Windows Media Player is Microsoft's equivalent of iTunes, a piece of software that handles the playback of music and video – not only on your PC, but any other compatible device on your network. It can also be used for creating playlists, transferring songs to portable media players and burning your own CDs.

It's a flexible piece of software, but not to be confused with the much more powerful Windows Media Center, which is no longer a core part of the operating system (see "Where's Media Center?", opposite).

MANAGING YOUR MUSIC In Windows 8, there are two ways of accessing your music collection. The new Music app (see p46), which you'll find pre-installed on the new Start screen, is a beautifully presented music player that also gives you access to the Xbox Music Store, where you'll find tens of thousands of albums for sale.

However, when it comes to managing your music collection you need something a little more powerful, which is where Windows Media Player steps in.

When you first open Windows Media Player – found by typing "Windows Media" from the Start screen – you should find that it has already imported and catalogued all the music and video stored on your PC. If you store your music in an unusual place on your PC, you might need to tell Windows Media Player where to find it. To do this, right-click on Music in the left-hand column, select Manage Music Library and add the folder where the music is stored.

If there are other switched-on PCs with media collections on your home network, you should see them listed under the Other Libraries section in the left-hand pane of Windows Media Player. Click on the PC's name and you should be able to access all the music and video stored on that device, as if it were stored on the hard disk of the computer in front of you.

CREATING AND BURNING PLAYLISTS You can create playlists of different tracks from the albums you've stored on your PC by clicking the Create Playlist button in the top menu bar. Give your Playlist a name, and you can then browse through the various albums on your computer and simply drag and drop the tracks you want to the name of the playlist in the left-hand pane. It's as easy as that.

If even that seems too much like hard work, you can get Windows Media Player to create playlists for you. Alongside the Create Playlist button you'll see a little down arrow: click that and select Create Auto Playlist. This allows you to generate playlists based on certain criteria. You might, for example, decide to create a playlist of all the songs in your media collection that you've rated at four stars or over. Alternatively, you could create a playlist of songs that you play most often at weekends; Windows Media Player has all this data stored and can create such lists in seconds.

Once you've finished creating a manual or auto playlist, you can burn the compilation of tracks to CD (provided you have a CD/DVD writer in your PC, of course). Click on the name of your playlist in the left-hand pane, then click on the Burn tab on the right-hand side of Windows Media Player and select Burn list. Click Start

Tip

Windows Media Player has a compact player mode that can sit quietly in the corner of the screen while you get on with other work. To activate compact mode, click on the little button with three squares and an arrow in the bottom right-hand corner of the Media Player window. In this mode, all you'll see is the album cover of the track being played and basic player controls. You can hit the button again to go back to the full player mode.

Creating playlists in **Windows Media Player** is a simple drag-and-drop operation.

Left: Windows Media Player can run in a corner of the screen, allowing you to carry on with other tasks.

Below left: the Media Player interface is easy to find your way around.

Below: Windows Media Center is no longer included with the operating system, but it can still be bought as an upgrade pack.

HOW LONG?
Getting started with Media Player and its features takes only a few minutes, but burning discs may take longer.

HOW HARD?
There's nothing particularly challenging about managing your media via Windows Media Player.

Burn and Windows will invite you to pop a blank CD into the drive, and calculate if it can squeeze all the music on to one CD, before starting to burn your disc. You can choose to burn individual albums as well as playlists.

MP3 PLAYERS Windows Media Player can also be used to synchronise your music collection with your MP3 player. Most MP3 players should be recognised automatically by Windows Media Player when plugged into your PC, with the exception of Apple's iPod devices, which are best managed using Apple's own iTunes software.

Synchronising music to your player is similar to the process for burning a CD. Click the Sync tab and create a list of music by dragging and dropping tracks or albums into the right-hand pane of Windows Media Player, then hit the Start Sync button.

DVD PLAYBACK You may have used Windows Media Player to watch DVDs on your PC in previous versions of Windows. Unfortunately, Microsoft has taken the decision to remove the DVD playback codecs from Windows 8, meaning that Windows Media Player can no longer handle the playback of commercial DVDs. The easiest way around this problem is to download a free, alternative media player called VLC Media Player from www.videolan.org/vlc. It shares many of the same features as Windows Media Player, and includes the crucial codecs (see p140 for more about DVD playback in Windows 8).

Where is Media Center?

For the past two editions of Windows, Windows Media Center has been built into the operating system. This can be used to view and record live television, as well as organise and play music and videos, all from a beautifully designed interface.

Windows Media Center hasn't been scrapped, but it's no longer included with Windows by default. Instead, Windows 8 users will have to pay for, download and install the separate Windows 8 Media Center Pack. Furthermore, this will only be available to users of Windows 8 Professional, not the Standard edition found on most home PCs.

At the time of publication, Microsoft hadn't announced the price of this upgrade pack, nor even completed the code or made it available for testing, so we can't tell you too much about it. What we can say, however, is that the Media Center Pack will support DVD playback, so those who use their Windows Media Center PC as an all-in-one entertainment system won't need to download another media player, such as VLC.

10

Entertainment

MICROSOFT'S NEW OPERATING SYSTEM AND THE XBOX CONSOLE WORK CLOSELY TOGETHER. FIND OUT HOW YOU CAN GET THE MOST OUT OF BOTH

Windows 8 and the Xbox 360

Technology companies often use the horrible word "ecosystem" to describe a range of devices that share common features and applications. In Microsoft's case, Windows 8 is joined at the hip with the company's Windows Phone devices and the Xbox games console, to form the so-called Windows ecosystem. It's the latter of those devices that we're going to focus on here.

XBOX SMARTGLASS The most impressive tie-up between Windows 8 and the Xbox 360 comes in the form of Windows SmartGlass. This is an app, downloadable for free from the Windows Store, that turns your tablet PC into a giant touch surface for controlling the console.

The Windows SmartGlass app makes it easy to open the apps you've installed on the Xbox console. Your most commonly used apps are displayed in tiles on the SmartGlass homescreen. This means you can, for example, click on the BBC iPlayer app, select a show to watch and start it playing, without even laying hands on your regular Xbox controller.

The SmartGlass has two modes: a regular tile-based interface that allows you to select what apps to use on the console, and the Xbox controller mode. This replicates the buttons found on your regular Xbox controller, allowing you to swish your finger left and right to scroll through the console's menus, and with "buttons" for the X, Y, A and B buttons found on your controller.

You can't actually play games with SmartGlass (frankly, we can't see why you'd want to, even if it were an option), but it does allow you to lie back on the sofa and browse the console's numerous non-gaming features.

XBOX LIVE GAMES The Windows 8 Games app is also tied in with the Xbox console (see p146). Not only does it allow you to play multiplayer games on your Windows 8 device using the Xbox Live service, it also provides details of your games, profile and achievements on the Xbox itself.

Start up the Games app on Windows 8 and, if you've signed into Windows 8 with the same Microsoft account linked to your Xbox Live profile, you should see your Xbox avatar. From that screen you can edit the appearance of your avatar, change your profile details and view your achievements in console games.

Swipe to the left and your Xbox Live friends' avatars should scroll into view. This shows you what game they're currently playing on their console, in case you fancy firing up the Xbox and joining them in a multiplayer session. Tap on the player's avatar and you can compare their achievements against yours in the games you both own.

If you return to the Games app homescreen and keep scrolling left, you'll also find sections for Xbox games you own and titles currently being sold in the Xbox store. For the games you currently own, you can click on an option to Explore the game, which provides details such

Tip

 If you're having problems getting your Xbox console to see your Windows 8 device, go into the console's Settings menu, select Console Settings and, under the Companion Device listing, make sure your Xbox is set to available.

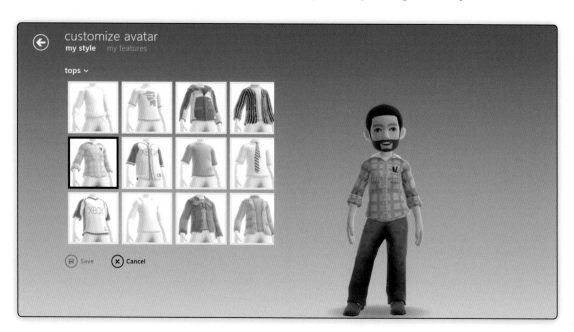

Modern Warfare® 3

overview   extras   achievements

related

overview

18
www.pegi.info
Bad Language
Violence

🛒 Buy game for Xbox 360

⚠ Play on Xbox 360

Set Beacon

2 friends recently played (1 online)

The Games on Demand version supports English. Modern Warfare® is back. The best-selling first person action series of all-time returns with the epic sequel to multiple "Game of the Year" award winner "Call of Duty®: Modern Warfare.

☰ View more

Details of your Xbox games can be viewed from your Windows 8 PC.

SmartGlass lets you open Xbox apps from your touchscreen tablet.

as your achievements within that game and any additional extras that are available for download, such as extra levels or add-ons that can be purchased. Here, you can also set a beacon, alerting your Xbox Live friends to the fact that you're online and open to a multiplayer challenge for the game in question. If any of your friends are currently playing the same game, they'll see a pop-up alert on their screen, letting them know you're available. You can even click a button to start playing the game on the Xbox console, although you'll either need to have installed it on your console or have the disc in the drive first.

MUSIC AND MOVIES So far, we've largely talked about accessing your Xbox from your PC, but it also works the other way around. There might be times, for example, when you're sitting in front of your games console and want to access content stored on your Windows 8 PC – your music collection, for example, or a movie.

As long as both your Xbox console and the PC in question are on and connected to the same home network (either via a wired or wireless connection), that's perfectly possible. Go to the Music Player app on your Xbox console, for example, and you should see the name of your Windows 8 PC listed in the available locations, underneath the Xbox's hard disk. Click on the name of your PC and you should be able to navigate the albums, artists or individual songs stored on your computer and play that content back through the console.

Similarly, open the Video Player app on your Xbox 360, and any video clips or movies stored on your computer should also be available for playback. It's a great way to watch movies edited on your PC on the big screen. The Xbox Music and Movie player will play back content stored in most popular media formats, such as MP3 and MPEG4 video. Bear in mind, however, that the console probably won't be able to access content that's protected by Digital Rights Management (DRM), such as Digital Copies of movies (see p141) stored on your PC.

Although the feature wasn't fully operational at the time of writing, you should also be able to play back content purchased in the Video and Music apps on your Windows 8 PC on your Xbox console, at the push of a button. That means if you've started watching a downloaded movie on your laptop on the train home from work, you can finish watching it on the big screen at home, picking up exactly where you left off.

If you're using the same login on both console and PC, all the setup has been performed for you.

HOW HARD?

The connection between Windows 8 and the Xbox is seamless, as long as you use the same Microsoft account on both devices.

WINDOWS 8 INTRODUCES A NEW TYPE OF GAME TO ADD TO THE TRADITIONAL PC GAMES WE'VE BEEN PLAYING FOR YEARS

Playing games

In the age of games consoles and iPads, the PC isn't the gaming powerhouse that it once was. However, the introduction of the Modern apps may help breathe new life into the Windows gaming market, and the traditional PC games-makers are far from finished. In this section, we'll explain what Windows 8 has to offer for hardcore and casual gamers alike.

MODERN GAMES If you click on the Store tile on the new Start screen, you'll notice a section of the app store devoted to games. The majority of titles you'll find in the Store are a new type of game for Windows 8. They have more in common with the lightweight game apps you might be used to from devices such as smartphones and tablets than traditional PC titles. Most will download in only a minute or two, and many are absolutely free.

If you do buy a game in the Windows Store, you'll be able to download and install it on all of your Windows 8 devices – PCs, laptops and tablets – up to a limit of five devices. Since these games are built on lightweight web technologies, they should run perfectly well on any device on which you install them (the exception to this being games labelled as Desktop, which we'll come on to later). You shouldn't have to pore over the recommended specifications, like you do with traditional PC games, to check that you have the right graphics card, grade of processor and sufficient memory. However, you can check for any special requirements before you pay for a game by checking the Details tab of its entry in the Windows Store.

As with any of the Modern apps in the Windows Store, you may be able to try a version of the game before you buy, allowing you to check that it runs smoothly on your tablet or PC first.

THE GAMES APP Aside from the games you can download from the Store, you should also find a Games app pre-installed on your Windows 8 device. This gives you access to another class of multiplayer game that allows you to compete against players all over the world, via Microsoft's Xbox Live service. Anybody with an Xbox console will already be familiar with Xbox Live, and if you've signed in to Windows with the same Microsoft account used for your Xbox console, you should see your Xbox avatar in the top right-hand corner of the screen.

In the section labelled Windows Games Store, you should find a selection of Windows 8 games that are playable against online opponents. Many of the early titles are Microsoft's own games, including revamped touch versions of Solitaire, Mahjong and Minesweeper. These all allow you to play in online challenges against both your Xbox Live friends and gamers from across the planet.

Tip

To get an experience similar to the Windows Store on the traditional Windows desktop, consider installing Steam (**http://store. steampowered.com**). This allows you to buy all your PC games from one central store, using the same payment details, and install those games on any PC you own. Steam is famed for its sales, which often offer huge discounts on relatively modern titles.

Windows 8 includes the usual traditional card games, such as FreeCell.

Wordament lets you pit your wits against players from all over the world.

Installing Modern games should take no time at all; desktop games can take much longer.

Installing and playing Modern Windows 8 games is a cinch; be a little more careful with desktop games.

In the Wordament game, which is very similar to the classic board game Boggle, you are given a set time period to find as many words as possible, and when the clock stops your score is compared to all the other players worldwide who are competing with the same set of letters as you. The satisfaction of finishing at the top of the world is immense.

The Games app also includes content related to Xbox console games that you are unable to play on your Windows 8 device.

DESKTOP GAMES Windows 8 also caters for the more hardcore gamer, allowing full x86 games to be installed on the traditional Windows desktop (except on Windows RT tablets). As ever, the Windows desktop games market spans from basic card games right through to the latest 3D action titles that are pushing the boundaries of graphics technology.

Microsoft will list traditional desktop games in the Windows Store – instead of a price or the word "free" in their listings, you will see them labelled with the word "desktop" – but they won't be as easy to buy and install as the new Modern games apps. You will have to follow the link to the publisher's website to pay for and download the game, and you won't be able to pay with one click using your Microsoft account.

You need to pay much closer attention to the required specifications when purchasing traditional desktop games compared to the new Modern apps, especially if you're running Windows 8 on a tablet or low-powered laptop. Many of the latest 3D games require high-powered, discrete graphics cards, which you will find only in desktop PCs and some very high-end laptops.

Similarly, keep an eye on processor, memory and hard disk space requirements. Tablet and laptop processors are normally built with longevity rather than raw power in mind, and may not be up to playing the latest

titles. Similarly, tablets and laptops that rely on solid-state drives (SSDs), rather than mechanical hard disks, will have limited storage space, and some games can demand hundreds of megabytes of free storage, which could easily swamp your system. Check the specifications carefully before making any purchase, as retailers are unlikely to refund you for purchasing a game that's beyond the capabilities of your system.

It's best to look for a game's "recommended specification" rather than "minimum specification". The minimum specification is the bare minimum it will take to make the game playable, but the experience is likely to be unsatisfactory if your computer just meets those base requirements, and you'll almost certainly be forced to sacrifice some graphic detail. The recommended specification is normally a much more reliable guide to the necessary hardware.

If you're not sure what hardware is in your system, you can find most of the details you need in the Windows Control Panel. The easiest way to access the necessary information is to go to the Windows Start screen, type "System", click on Settings in the right-hand panel below the search field, and click on the entry marked System. Here you'll find details of your processor and memory, while the Device Manager option on the left will display your graphics card under the Display Settings entry.

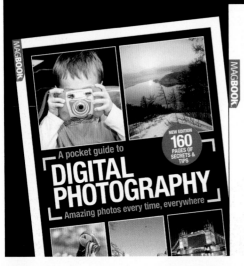
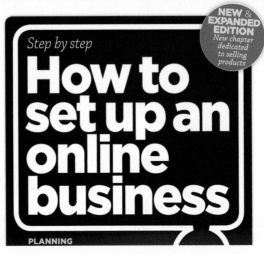

WHETHER LIVE TILES ARE TRIPPING YOU UP OR SKYDRIVE HAS YOU GROUNDED, YOU'LL FIND EVERYTHING YOU NEED TO POLISH UP YOUR PC KNOWLEDGE HERE.

Windows jargon explained

32-BIT/64-BIT Refers to either the processor or the type of operating system. Most modern hardware is 64-bit.

802.11 The name of the official standard that governs aspects of wireless networking and hardware. 802.11b, 802.11g and 802.11n denote the three types of consumer wireless connections. 802.11b is the oldest and slowest, 802.11g is faster, and 802.11n is faster still and now the norm for all new equipment. A new, faster standard called 802.11ac has just appeared on the market, but at present is supported by few devices.

A

ADSL (ASYMMETRIC DIGITAL SUBSCRIBER LINE) The most common form of broadband internet connection, working over traditional phone lines. Regular ADSL offers maximum speeds of up to 24Mbits/sec. The major alternatives are cable or fibre-optic broadband, which can offer speeds of up to 100Mbits/sec or beyond in neighbourhoods served by cable or fibre broadband equipment.

APPS/APPLICATIONS The new-style programs that are downloaded from the Windows 8 Store are generally referred to as "apps", while full-blown desktop software packages are more typically referred to as "applications". In effect, though, they mean the same thing.

B

BIOS The Basic Input/Output System configures your motherboard at startup and boots your PC. It's stored on a flash memory chip on the motherboard; its settings can be accessed by holding down a specified key during startup.

BITLOCKER/BITLOCKER TO GO BitLocker and BitLocker To Go are only found in the premium editions of Windows. BitLocker was introduced in Windows Vista as a way to encrypt an entire hard disk, making it all but impossible for laptop thieves to access the owner's data. BitLocker To Go applies the same principle to external disks, such as USB flash drives.

BLU-RAY The successor to DVD, storing up to nine hours of high-definition video or 50GB of data on a disc.

BREADCRUMB BAR (OR BREADCRUMB TRAIL) A navigation aid in Windows Explorer; each "crumb" shows a folder

you've clicked through to reach your present location, and clicking on one takes you directly back to that folder.

C

CHARMS A new concept for Windows 8, charms provide access to functions such as Search, Devices and Settings. They are accessed on touchscreen devices by swiping from the right-hand edge of the screen, or by hovering the mouse in the bottom right corner. See our guide on p34.

CPU (CENTRAL PROCESSING UNIT) Also known simply as a processor, the CPU is the component that interprets and executes computer programs. Common CPUs in personal computers include Intel's Core i3, i5 and i7 series and AMD's FX range.

D

DESKTOP The Windows desktop used to be the primary working area of a PC. It's now been relegated in favour of the new Start screen, but it's still a vital part of Windows for those who use desktop software. It is accessed by clicking on the Desktop tile on the Windows 8 Start screen.

DIRECTX A set of Windows extensions from Microsoft designed to accelerate games and other performance-hungry software by allowing them to use your PC's graphics hardware to the full.

DUAL BOOT It's entirely possible to run two OSes on one computer – for example, if you wish to keep Windows 7 but use Windows 8 as your main environment. You don't even need two hard disks to make this work.

DVB-T (DIGITAL VIDEO BROADCASTING – TERRESTRIAL) A standard used by Freeview digital TV in the UK, enabling digital TV tuner cards and USB sticks to receive digital programmes through a regular rooftop aerial. DVB-T2 tuners can also receive Freeview HD channels.

F

FAT32 A hard disk format used by older operating systems such as Windows 98 and also devices such as USB flash drives. Windows 8 can happily read and write FAT32 drives, but the more advanced NTFS format is more reliable and is now the standard for hard disks.

FIREWALL Software or hardware designed to protect networks and PCs from hackers, or from the malicious software that they control. Windows 8 has its own firewall built into the operating system, so there's no desperate need to purchase a third-party option.

FIREWIRE Also known as IEEE-1394 or iLink, this is a high-speed method of connecting external devices such as MiniDV camcorders. It's an alternative to USB, but more popular on the Apple Mac than in the PC world.

FLASH MEMORY A type of RAM used in USB memory drives and the memory cards for digital cameras. Flash memory retains its data even when power is removed.

FULL-DISK ENCRYPTION A system that encrypts all of the data on a disk, making it impossible for a potential hacker to gain access to the information on it without the password. The encryption may be enforced by a dedicated processor embedded on a PC's motherboard (called a Trusted Platform Module or TPM chip). BitLocker, included with the Professional version of Windows 8, is the brand name of Microsoft's full-disk encryption technology.

G

GIGABYTE (GB) 1,024 megabytes when referred to in the context of RAM; 1,000 megabytes in the context of hard disks. No one said this would be easy.

GPU (GRAPHICS PROCESSING UNIT) The chip in your PC, either built into your motherboard or onto a graphics card, that handles 3D games and drives your screen display.

H

HARD DISK A form of storage that usually holds all of the data stored permanently within your PC. Usually these are based on spinning magnetic disks inside a metal case, but the newest and fastest drives use memory chips instead: these are known as solid-state drives, or SSDs.

HDCP (HIGH-DEFINITION CONTENT PROTECTION) A form of DRM (digital rights management) used to ensure that PCs and related equipment can play, but not copy, high-definition (HD) media such as Blu-ray movies.

HDMI (HIGH-DEFINITION MULTIMEDIA INTERFACE) A connector designed to carry video and audio signals between high-definition devices.

HDTV 720P, 1080I, 1080P High-definition film and television standards, specifying how much information is encoded in a movie clip or TV show. The numbers refer to the number of horizontal lines in a picture, and whether those lines are interlaced (i) or progressive (p). Higher numbers are better, and "p" is better than "i".

HOMEGROUP HomeGroup is Microsoft's name for a technology that allows you to quickly and easily share files and devices between all the PCs and laptops on your home network, even if the printer (for example) is connected to a different PC. See p94.

I

INTERNET EXPLORER Microsoft's web browser. Windows 8 comes with two different versions of Internet Explorer 10 pre-installed, one geared for the new Modern-style UI, and another version for the regular Windows desktop. Many people prefer alternative browsers, such as Google's Chrome or Mozilla's Firefox.

IP ADDRESS A number assigned to a PC on a network to allow it to be identified, so that incoming data can find its way to the correct computer.

ISP (INTERNET SERVICE PROVIDER) A company that provides internet access to end users.

J

JUMP LISTS A feature introduced in Windows 7, Jump Lists is Microsoft's term for the dozen or so recently accessed documents that spring to life when you right-click on a program icon on the Taskbar. Software makers can add extra features to Jump Lists, too; for instance, Microsoft's Media Player lets you access playback controls straight from its Jump List. See p70.

L

LIBRARIES A concept introduced with Windows 7, there are four different types of Library by default: Documents, Music, Pictures and Video. Even if you store your music in several different places on your PC or network, you can access all of it from the Music Library. See p104.

LIVE TILES Live tiles on the new Windows 8 Start screen display information from the relevant app. The live tile for the Calendar app, for example, displays details of forthcoming appointments. See p32.

LOCAL Describes a folder, file or resource that's stored within or connected directly to the PC you're using, rather than on a network or another computer.

M

MEDIA CENTER Microsoft's simple-to-use application for viewing photos and video, watching TV and for listening to music. Designed to work with a remote control, but can also be controlled via the mouse and keyboard. Media Center is at its most powerful when teamed up in a PC with a TV tuner. See p142.

MEDIA CENTER EXTENDER A device, such as the Xbox 360, that can connect to your Windows 8 PC over a network and output all the music, video and TV stored on it directly to a television or hi-fi.

MEDIA STREAMING See streaming.

METRO Metro was the working codename for the new interface for Windows 8. After a legal challenge, Microsoft decided to drop the Metro name and now refers to it as the Modern UI.

MODERN UI See Metro (above).

MULTITOUCH The capability for a computer or another interactive device (most famously, Apple's iPhone) to translate two or more finger touches into a command. For example, pinch two fingers together on a Windows 8 touchscreen PC and the picture will zoom out. Drag your fingers apart on the screen and the photo will zoom in.

N

NTFS (NEW TECHNOLOGY FILE SYSTEM) A hard disk format used in Windows NT, 2000, XP, Vista and Windows 7 and 8. The successor to FAT.

O

OEM (ORIGINAL EQUIPMENT MANUFACTURER) The manufacturer of an entire PC or an individual component. You can buy so-called OEM versions of equipment and software, including Windows, which are cheaper but will come without manuals or technical support.

OPTICAL DRIVE A catch-all term for CD, DVD and Blu-ray disc drives.

P

PARENTAL CONTROLS A software system that monitors and controls how your children use your computer. Typically, parental controls will restrict internet access to specified times and websites, and limit which applications can be run. Windows 8 has parental controls built in – read our guide to setting them up on p116.

PARTITIONS Artificially segregated areas of a hard disk. If you create two partitions, it's possible to install two different versions of Windows (or any other operating system), one on each partition.

PICTURE PASSWORDS A new way of accessing your Windows 8 PC by tapping or swiping on predefined areas of a photo on-screen, as opposed to entering a regular password.

R

RAM (RANDOM ACCESS MEMORY) A high-speed form of memory holding the data and documents that you're currently using. The contents of RAM are lost when the PC is switched off (except in the case of flash RAM).

S

SAVED SEARCHES Folders that contain a set of user-defined search results, which update dynamically as files matching the criteria are added.

SECURE BOOT A new feature in Windows 8 that prevents unauthorised operating systems from running on your computer. See p82.

SKYDRIVE SkyDrive is a free Microsoft service that gives you gigabytes of free online storage. You can access SkyDrive through the app built into the Windows 8 Start screen or via the revamped Windows Explorer. See our guide to SkyDrive on p106.

START SCREEN The traditional Windows Start button is no more. In its place comes a new Start screen, replete with big colourful tiles for all the apps and traditional desktop applications installed on your PC.

STREAMING If you want to listen to a piece of music stored on one computer on another, the simplest method is to "stream" it. Rather than copy the file and save it on the new PC, this process sends the music bit by bit; when you've finished listening, any information is automatically deleted from the receiving PC. If you ever use services such as BBC iPlayer, this uses a similar technology.

SYSTEM RESTORE A way to "roll back" Windows to a previously saved set of settings. By default, Windows 8 takes a snapshot of settings whenever a major change occurs, such as the addition of new hardware. See p110.

SYSTEM TRAY A small area at the right of the Taskbar that's used to show volume settings, network status, and other applications that are running in the background.

T

TABLET PC A slate-style mobile computer that may or may not include a keyboard, but largely relies on a touchscreen for navigation and data input. Can also refer to a laptop that includes a touchscreen in addition to a keyboard.

TASKBAR Arranged by default along the bottom of the desktop, the Taskbar is home to the System Tray, as well as the Taskbar icons of programs that are currently running or "pinned" to the Taskbar. See p66.

TCP/IP (TRANSMISSION CONTROL PROTOCOL/INTERNET PROTOCOL) A set of protocols used to transmit data over networks; the fundamental protocols at the heart of the internet. Windows 8 normally configures TCP/IP settings automatically, so you shouldn't need to worry about it.

U

UAC (USER ACCOUNT CONTROL) A security feature of Windows 8 that prevents software from making major changes to your programs and settings without your explicit authorisation. See p124.

USB (UNIVERSAL SERIAL BUS) A "plug and play" interface that's used to connect the vast majority of peripherals to a PC. Comes in three versions: the original USB 1 connector runs at 12Mbits/sec, while the upgraded USB 2 can carry a much faster 480Mbits/sec over the same cables. The latest version, USB 3, supports transfers of 4,800Mbits/sec using new "SuperSpeed" cables.

V

VHD (VIRTUAL HARD DISK) A file format that represents the contents of a virtual hard drive, typically used to run another instance of an operating system on a PC. See p76.

W

WAN (WIDE AREA NETWORK) A network that extends over a large geographical area, as opposed to a LAN (local area network). A broadband modem's external connection (to the internet) is referred to as a WAN.

WEP (WIRED EQUIVALENT PRIVACY) A common, but flawed, method of encrypting the data sent over a Wi-Fi connection. It gives fair protection but can be broken by a determined eavesdropper. See WPA.

WI-FI The generic term for wireless networks and connections based on the 802.11a, 802.11b, 802.11g and 802.11n standards.

WINDOWS EXPLORER The built-in way to browse your files (and your network) in Windows. Not to be confused with Internet Explorer, which is used for web browsing.

WPA (WI-FI PROTECTED ACCESS) A very secure method of encrypting the data transmitted on a wireless network – you should use this in preference to WEP wherever possible. The WPA2 standard is even tougher again.

WINDOWS RT The version of Windows designed to run on ARM processors, rather than the x86 (often Intel-made) processors normally found in PCs. Will be installed predominantly on tablet devices.

The Ultimate Guide to Windows 8

EDITORIAL

Editor
Barry Collins

Designer
Colette Fahy

Sub Editors
Martin James, Steve Haines

Digital Production Manager
Nicky Baker +44 20 7907 6056

Original design and layout
Adam Banks adam@adambanks.com

Contributors
David Bayon, Jonathan Bray, Darien Graham-Smith, Mike Jennings

MANAGEMENT +44 20 7907 6000

MagBook Publisher
Dharmesh Mistry

Operations Director
Robin Ryan

MD of Advertising
Julian Lloyd-Evans

Editorial Director
Tim Danton

Newstrade Director
David Barker

Chief Operating Officer
Brett Reynolds

Group Finance Director
Ian Leggett

Chief Executive
James Tye

Chairman
Felix Dennis

LICENSING & SYNDICATION

Licensing
Carlotta Serantoni +44 20 7907 6550
(carlotta_serantoni@dennis.co.uk)

Syndication
Anj Dosaj Halai +44 20 7907 6132
(anj_dosaj-halai@dennis.co.uk)

Index

3G, 8, 98
802.11, 94
64-bit versions, 15
Accessibility, 88
Action Center, 118-119
Airplane Mode, 6, 98
Armed, 56
AVG Anti-Virus, 127
Awesome Picture, 58
Backup, 112-113
Barcode Generator, 59
Battery management, 86
Bing Maps, 52
Bing Search, 53
BitDefender Internet Security, 128
BitLocker, 78
BitLocker To Go, 78
Blu-ray playback, 140
Boot times, 9
Calendar, 45
Camera, 48
Charms 34-35
Clean installation, 111
Cocktail Flow, 57
Data plans, 98
Digital Copies, 140
Disk images, 76
DVD playback, 140, 143
Encyclopaedia Britannica, 58
Eset Smart Security, 128
Facebook, 40, 44
Family Safety, 116-117
Feed Reader, 59
File handling, 102-103
File History, 112-113
Finance, 51
Fine Cooking, 57
Flash Cards, 58
Flickr, 40, 44
Flight Aware, 56
Folders, 102-103
Fresh Paint, 58
F-Secure Internet Security, 128
Games, 146
Gmail, 44
Growth Tracker, 59
Handbrake, 141
Handwriting recognition, 134-135
HomeGroup, 96-97
Installing Modern apps, 55
Installing Windows 8, 19-21

Internet Explorer 10, 92-93
ISOs, 8, 76
Jump Lists, 70
Kaspersky Internet Security, 128
Kindle, 57
Kinect, 9
Libraries, 104-105
LinkedIn, 44
Live tiles, 6, 33, 37
Lock screen, 7, 36
McAfee Internet Security, 128
Magnifier, 88
Mahjong, 146
Mail, 44
Maintenance, 119
Metro Twit, 56
Microsoft Hotmail, 44
Microsoft Surface, 23
Minesweeper, 146
Ministry of Sound, 56
Mobile broadband, 98
Mouse Keys, 89
Movies, 47
MP3 players, 143
MSN, 44
Music, 46
Music Maker Jam, 58
National Rail Enquiries, 58
News, 50
Norton Internet Security, 129
Office 2013, 22
OneNote MX, 58
Onscreen keyboards, 6, 136-137
Outlook.com, 44
Panoramic wallpapers, 9
Parental controls, 116-117
People, 45
Personalisation, 36
Photos, 48
Picture passwords, 8, 40
Pinball FX2, 57
Playlists, 142
PowerDVD, 140
Power Plans, 86
Refresh PC 8, 80, 110
Reinstalling Windows, 111
Reset PC, 8, 80
Ribbon, 64
Safe Mode, 81
Search 8, 34-35
Secure Boot, 8, 82

Semantic Zoom, 32
Settings, 30
Shortcuts, 68
SIM cards, 98
SkyDrive, 6, 106-107
Sky News, 57
SmartGlass, 144
Snap to edges, 68
Solitaire, 146
Sport, 50
SSIDs, 94
Start screen, 28-29, 32
Synchronisation, 8
System Restore, 81
Taskbar, 66
Task Manager, 6, 71
Task Switcher, 69
Themes, 67
Touchscreen gestures, 132-133
Touchpads, 133
Travel, 51
Trend Micro Titanium, 129
Troubleshooting, 111
Update Star, 115
USB 3, 9
User accounts, 8, 38-39
User Account Control, 124-125
VHDs, 76
VLC Media Player, 140, 143
Wikipedia, 57
Windows 7 upgrades, 18
Windows 8 Pro, 14
Windows Defender, 118, 120-121
Windows desktop, 62-63
Windows Explorer, 8, 64-65
Windows Firewall, 118, 122-123
Windows Games Store, 146
Windows Live Mail, 44
Windows Media Center, 143
Windows Media Player, 142-143
Windows Peek, 69
Windows RT, 16, 22
Windows Shake, 68
Windows Store, 54
Windows To Go, 84
Windows Update, 114
WinDVD Pro, 140
Wi-Fi network, 94-95
Wordament, 147
Xbox 360, 144
Xbox Live, 145